DON'T BE A DUMMY

To George,

After you read my book, you will understand all of the mistakes your opponents are making. Enjoy!

Elliot Steinfeld

Don't Be a DUMMY

*HOW TO BID, DEFEND AND
DECLARE A BRIDGE HAND
LIKE AN EXPERT*

Elliot Sternlicht

To order additional copies of this book, contact:
Xlibris Corporation
1-888-795-4274
www.Xlibris.com
Orders@Xlibris.com

15885-STER

CONTENTS

ACKNOWLEDGMENTS 9

FOREWORD 11

PREFACE 13

AUTHOR'S MESSAGE...15

CHAPTER 1 17
    BASIC PLAYING STYLE

CHAPTER 2 37
    DISTRIBUTION

CHAPTER 3 60
    BIDDING PRINCIPLES YOUR MOTHER NEVER
    TAUGHT YOU

CHAPTER 4 76
    MORE BIDDING PRINCIPLES

CHAPTER 5 112
    TYPES OF DOUBLES

CHAPTER 6 150
    DECLARER PLAY

CHAPTER 7 186
    DEFENSE

CHAPTER 8 232
    MATCHPOINT STRATEGY

CHAPTER 9 264
    GREAT BRIDGE HANDS

Index 277

I would like to dedicate this book to Harold Berlin,
a great bridge player who taught me what bridge is all about,
to my sweet and loving parents Manny and Madeline,
and to my wonderful wife Betty.

ACKNOWLEDGMENTS

As a first-time bridge author, I would like to acknowledge other authors whose ideas I have used in this book. Specifically, I have based my description of the Law of Total Trumps on Larry Cohen's book, *To Bid or Not to Bid: The Law of Total Tricks*. The Obvious Shift Principle is derived from the Granovetters' book, *A Switch in Time*. Some of the competitive bidding ideas discussed in this book are based on Kit Woolsey's book, *Matchpoints*, and on Marshall Miles' book, *Stronger Competitive Bidding*.

I am also indebted to Harold Feldheim, Hugh Kelsey, Eddie Kantar and Frank Stewart, great bridge players who have also written many excellent bridge books. I have drawn on some of their ideas in presenting some of the concepts in this book. I would especially like to thank Zia Mahmood for writing the introduction to the book.

I would like to thank everyone who assisted me in reviewing this book and checking the material for accuracy. I am especially grateful to Riva Akerman, Robert Kuhnreich, Sandy Levine, Barry Rigal, Madeline Sternlicht and Manny Sternlicht. The contributions made by these individuals have been invaluable.

Elliot Sternlicht

FOREWORD

I have known the author Elliot for some years. He works at the Regency Whist Club in New York, and he fills in as a house player in my rubber bridge game there. He is one of my favorite house players, and is a welcome addition to the game.

When Elliot told me he was writing a bridge book and asked me to write the introduction, I told him, "If you actually write a book, I will be happy to do it." Most of the time, when people talk about writing a bridge book, it never actually gets done, so I didn't give it much further thought.

Six months later, Elliot handed me a completed copy of his book, and asked me if I would still write the introduction. I was impressed that he had actually completed a book, and I agreed to take a look at it. I was even more impressed at how good a book it is. There is excellent bridge advice to be found in this book for every level of player. The ideas are clearly written in an easy-to-understand fashion, and the bridge hands that are used in the book, which are actual tournament hands, are excellent examples. I would recommend this book to any bridge player who is interested in improving his or her game. After which, perhaps you would like to join me at the rubber bridge table.

Zia Mahmood

PREFACE

The primary purpose of this book is to provide bridge players with advanced bridge concepts without having to learn them the hard way by getting bad results against more experienced players. I have tried to share some bridge principles that I have learned in over twenty years of playing tournament bridge in this book. This is a good way for intermediate and advanced bridge players to acquire a modicum of bridge expertise without getting this knowledge from the bridge version of the school of hard knocks.

A secondary purpose of this book is to entertain my fellow bridge players with some of the most fascinating hands that I have encountered in twenty years of playing bridge at national and regional tournaments. Most of the deals presented in this book actually took place in a tournament between 1984–2002. I have used these fascinating hands to illustrate certain bridge principles that I have learned from experience.

Regardless of your current level of bridge, you will find this book to be both instructive and entertaining. I hope that you get as much enjoyment out of reading this book as I got out of writing it.

Elliot Sternlicht

AUTHOR'S MESSAGE

When I first started playing in tournaments sponsored by the American Contract Bridge League (ACBL), there was no such thing as stratified pairs. Everybody played against everybody else, and you learned how to play bridge by going up against tough bridge players and learning from the school of "hard knocks". I learned how to play bridge by taking my lumps from more experienced tournament players, and I wouldn't trade that experience for anything. It is a real shame that nowadays you can make Life Master without ever playing in a Flight A or Open event!

As I was developing as a bridge player, I learned certain principles from bitter experience. For example, if you make a preemptive bid and the opponents confidently bid to 3NT, do not lead your suit unless you have a strong sequence. After a few humbling occasions when I led from a broken suit, which gave away a trick and resulted in a poor score for us, I developed this principle. I remember wishing that somebody could formulate some bridge principles that I could learn from without having to learn everything the hard way.

It is with that goal in mind that I have written this book. I have been composing this book in my mind for quite some time. Part of this book imparts certain bridge principles that I have learned in over twenty years of intensive bridge play. These principles relate to all three aspects of bridge – bidding, declarer play and defense. Part of this book is based on bridge lessons that I have been giving for the past ten years. Some material is the result of the practical advice that I have imparted to my clients who are seeking to improve their game. Part of the book gives a detailed explanation of popular conventions, including examples of when they should be used. There is a summary of the key points and a quiz at the end of each chapter to test your understanding of the concepts that were discussed in that chapter.

Since I started playing in tournaments, I have always saved the hand records that are distributed after the game. The vast majority of the hands shown in this book are based on actual hands that came up in tournament play.

The bidding in the book assumes that both partners are playing a two-over-one, game-forcing bidding style, with five-card majors, forcing notrump, weak two bids, negative doubles, and limit raises in the majors and inverted raises in the minors. Certain abbreviations in the book are standard, as follows:

T	= Ten
RHO	= Right Hand Opponent
LHO	= Left Hand Opponent
DBL	= Double
RDBL	= Redouble
NT	= Notrump

All of the suggestions in the book are based on my bridge experiences and have worked well for me. You, the reader, should read this book with an open mind. Whether or not you adopt the concepts that I recommend in this book, I believe that reading this book will improve your game and introduce you to many new concepts about bridge.

Elliot Sternlicht
January 2003

CHAPTER 1

BASIC PLAYING STYLE

A. Opening Bids

In order to open the bidding at the one-level, there are two requirements:

1) At least two quick tricks*.
2) A convenient rebid.

Here are some hands where my advice on whether you should or should not open the bidding may surprise you:

HAND A	HAND B	HAND C	HAND D
♠ QJ8632	♠ K	♠ AQJ85	♠ A54
♥ Q	♥ Q74	♥ QT7653	♥ 53
♦ A964	♦ AQ53	♦ K5	♦ AQT975
♣ QJ	♣ J9754	♣ —	♣ 76

Hand A should pass in first or second seat – you have only one quick trick, your singleton queen of hearts is of dubious value, and your spade suit is not good enough to open with a weak two bid.

* Quick tricks are calculated as follows:

A = 1 quick trick   AQ = 1 ½ quick tricks
Kx = ½ quick trick   KQ = 1 quick trick
AK = 2 quick tricks

Opening the bidding 1♠ on this type of hand may well lead to disaster. Hand B is another hand that should not open the bidding – you have only one and one-half quick tricks and a questionable value in the singleton king of spades, and you also have a rebid problem if you open 1♣ and your partner responds 1♠.

Hand C is an opening bid, but you should open the bidding 1♠ and treat the hand as 5-5 in the majors. You are not strong enough to open 1♥ and reverse into 2♠ opposite a 1NT response from your partner. Hand D is a 1♦ opening bid – you have two and one-half quick tricks and an easy rebid.

Notice that I recommend that you pass with Hands A and B, both of which contain twelve high card points, and open the bidding with Hand D, which contains just ten high card points. Success at bridge is measured by how many tricks your side can take, not by how many points you happen to hold. Use the point count as a guide, but do not become a slave to point count.

When you have a marginal opening hand, you should look at two factors: 1) High card points in your long suits; 2) Length in spades - with a marginal opening bid, you should pass with spade shortness but open the bidding with spade length. A famous British expert named Jonathan Cansino invented the Cansino count to determine whether or not to open the bidding in fourth position. The Cansino count works as follows: Add your high card points plus the number of spades you have in your hand. If this total is fifteen or more, you should open the bidding, but if the total is less than fifteen, you should pass the hand out.

Here are some examples of hands with bidding problems:

HAND 1	HAND 2	HAND 3	HAND 4
♠ 5	♠ 64	♠ A85	♠ K64
♥ KJ95	♥ 75	♥ T4	♥ Q743
♦ AQ976	♦ AKT6	♦ KQ74	♦ K63
♣ K82	♣ AJ963	♣ AJ63	♣ A82

Hands 1 and 2 both have rebid problems. On Hand 1, you must be prepared for partner to respond 1♠ to your 1♦ opening bid. In this case, your best rebid is 1NT, showing a balanced minimum. Obviously, you are not strong enough to reverse into 2♥, and rebidding 1NT with a singleton in responder's suit is much preferable to rebidding a five-card minor suit.

Some of you may be wondering what is wrong with rebidding 2♦ with a five-card suit, since you only promised three diamonds with your 1♦ opening bid. The problem with rebidding a five-card minor suit is that if your partner passes, you are playing in the **lowest scoring partscore**. The other players who rebid 1NT have the advantage of playing in the highest scoring partscore. In addition, having the agreement that rebidding your own suit promises a six-card or longer suit makes subsequent bidding by the responder easier to manage. For example, the responder can raise your minor suit to the three-level, inviting a game, with Kx, knowing that there is a good chance of taking six tricks in this suit. If your 2♦ rebid only promises a five-card suit, the responder is frequently guessing what bid to make.

On Hand 2, if you open 1♣ and your partner responds 1♥ or 1♠, what will your rebid be? You do not have a good rebid – rebidding 2♣ on just a five-card suit is losing strategy, as we have just discussed, and rebidding 1NT with two small doubletons is also not a good bid. To avoid this rebid problem, it is reasonable to open 1♦ and rebid 2♣ over partner's expected 1♥ or 1♠ response.

On Hand 3, you are probably thinking, "What is the problem? I can open 1♦ and I can rebid 1NT if partner responds 1♥ or 1♠." The problem is that partner might hold either of the following hands:

HAND A	HAND B
♠ K63	♠ J63
♥ 983	♥ 983
♦ 52	♦ 5
♣ KT975	♣ KQT754

Over a 1♦ opening, partner is forced to respond 1NT, and you miss your club fit. If the opponents overcall in a major suit, your partner is not strong enough to mention his club suit over a 1♦ opening bid. I have never understood why players open 1♦ with this hand instead of 1♣. Since you intend to rebid 1NT over a major suit response, why not open the lower ranking minor in case partner has a weak hand with length in clubs? The only effect of opening 1♦ with 4-4 in the minor suits is that it makes it difficult for your side to get to a club fit if you have one! If you are in third seat, you would tend to open your better minor suit in order to direct a lead from your partner, but in first and second seats, opening 1♣ is a more flexible call with four cards in each minor.

Hand 4, with twelve points, should be passed in first and second seats – if your partner cannot open the bidding, there is no game for your side. The problem with opening flat twelve-point hands such as this one is that your side invariably gets too high in the bidding if your partner has a good hand. Another way of looking at it is that if you pass initially with this hand, you can subsequently bid very aggressively, since partner realizes that you are a passed hand. If you open the bidding, however, you spend the rest of the auction apologizing to partner for opening with such minimum values.

In third and fourth seat, the Cansino count is fifteen (twelve points plus three spades), so you should open Hand 4 in either of these positions. You should pass any response your partner makes, since you have no interest in game opposite a passed hand.

A good rule of hand evaluation is to **subtract one point for 4-3-3-3 distribution**. Thus, if you are playing fifteen- to seventeen-point notrumps, you should open 1NT with a 4-3-3-3 eighteen count, and you should open 1 of a minor and rebid 1NT with a flat fifteen-point hand, treating it as **less than a 1NT opening bid**. Here are some examples of using this hand evaluation technique:

HAND A	HAND B	HAND C
♠ K75	♠ A96	♠ AT96
♥ J43	♥ K75	♥ K4
♦ A62	♦ KQJ4	♦ QJT6
♣ AK92	♣ AJ2	♣ KJ9

With Hand A, you should open 1♣ and rebid 1NT if partner responds 1♦, 1♥ or 1♠. With flat distribution and no intermediate spot cards, treat this hand as a minimum balanced hand **less than a 1NT opening**. With Hand B, you should open 1NT despite holding eighteen points, again deducting one point for the flat distribution and lack of intermediates. With Hand C, open 1NT – although you have only fourteen points, you have excellent spot cards. Your tens and nines, although they do not count for anything in the point count, will enable your hand to take extra tricks in notrump.

B. Weak Two Bids

There are two approaches towards playing weak two bids:

1) Disciplined – You promise a good six-card suit with two of the top three or three of the top five honors.

2) Destructive – Your suit is of random quality, and may only be a five-card suit. Your primary purpose for opening a weak two bid is to interfere with the opponents' auction.

My distinct preference is to play disciplined weak two bids in first and second seats, at any vulnerability. When you play disciplined weak two bids, the responder is able to judge accurately how high to bid and whether or not to defend if the opponents compete in the auction. This ability to judge how high to compete is critical in a competitive auction.

Remember that a weak two bid not only preempts your opponents, but also takes up valuable bidding space from your partner if he happens to be the one holding a good hand. For this reason, **preempts are most effective in first and third seats.** In first seat, there are two opponents and only one partner to preempt, so the odds are in your favor. In third seat, your partner has already passed, so the odds are strongly in favor of your opponent in fourth seat having a good hand. Second seat is the worst seat to preempt, because one of your opponents is already a passed hand. There is a 50-50 chance that your partner holds a strong hand. For this reason, **second seat weak two bids should be pure in every respect**, with no flaws to the hand. Some flaws that a weak two bid opening could have would be poor spot cards in your suit, a side four-card suit, or three cards in the other major.

Ideally, a weak two bid should contain a good six-card suit, with the majority of the points in that suit. You can have one outside feature (an ace or a king), and you should generally not have a four-card major suit on the side.

Let us take a look at some hands that should or should not open with a weak two bid:

HAND A	HAND B	HAND C	HAND D
♠ AQT962	♠ K53	♠ QT7	♠ T98653
♥ 73	♥ KJT986	♥ AT9	♥ A76
♦ K94	♦ A5	♦ KJT954	♦ Q4
♣ 85	♣ 97	♣ 3	♣ K6

Hand A is a classic 2♠ opening – you have a good six-card suit, with just one outside feature. Hand B should open the bidding 1♥ – when you have a good six-card suit and two outside features, the hand should be opened at the one-level. Hand C should not be opened 2♦ in first or second seats – although you have a good six-card diamond suit, you have good support for both major suits, and you could easily miss a major suit partscore (or even game) if you open 2♦. Hand D is the opposite of what a weak two bid should look like. Instead of a good six-card suit with most of your points in that suit, Hand D features a poor six-card suit with all of your points outside of the suit. How can your partner possibly know what to do if you open 2♠ on both Hand A and Hand D? Opening 2♠ on a poor suit and outside values is losing bridge tactics, and you should just pass with this hand.

The main advantage of playing disciplined weak two bids is that partner can confidently bid a game with some values and a doubleton honor in your suit. Here is an illustrative example:

Opener	Responder
♠ 863	♠ KQJ
♥ AJT982	♥ Q6
♦ KT2	♦ QJ64
♣ J	♣ A853

When the opener bids 2♥, the responder can ask for a feature by bidding 2NT. When the opener shows a diamond feature, the responder can confidently jump to 4♥. If the heart finesse wins, declarer will make eleven tricks, and if the finesse loses, declarer still makes ten tricks and a game.

Responding to A Weak Two Bid

In order to try for game over a weak two bid, the responder must have **better** than an opening bid. With a singleton or a void in partner's suit, you should almost always pass, unless you have an exceptionally strong hand. The greater the fit you have in your partner's suit, the fewer points you need to try for game.

With a fit in your partner's suit, you should always raise your partner's suit, **regardless of how many points you have.** Remember that if you have a weak hand and your partner also has a weak hand, the opponents can make a lot of tricks in their long suit. By raising your partner's suit with a fit, you take up precious bidding room from your opponents when they have the majority of the points.

Here are some examples of responding to your partner's weak two bid. In each case, your partner has opened the bidding 2♠, and your RHO has passed:

HAND A	HAND B	HAND C	HAND D
♠ Q74	♠ 3	♠ 3	♠ 7532
♥ JT	♥ 4	♥ AQ74	♥ 974
♦ KJ83	♦ AKQT96	♦ KJ52	♦ 3
♣ Q874	♣ AQJ97	♣ K984	♣ QJT75

With Hand A, you should raise your partner to 3♠. Raising your partner's weak two bid is **non-forcing**, and makes it tougher for your opponents to get into the bidding. If you pass 2♠, it is very easy for your LHO to bid 3♥ – the opponents probably have at least eight hearts between them. Bidding 3♠ makes it much tougher for your opponents to compete. **You should always raise your partner's weak two bid with a fit**, in order to make life difficult for your opponents.

With Hand B, you should bid 3♦. Most players play that a new suit over a weak two bid by an unpassed hand is forcing for one round. If partner rebids 3♠, you will bid 4♣, showing a strong two-suited hand.

Hands C and D are opposite sides of the coin. Hand C has points but no fit, and you should pass your partner's 2♠ bid without any hesitation. You hope the opponents will balance, and you will happily double anything they bid. However, if you think for a long time and then pass, the opponents will know to stay out of the auction. You must pass in tempo when you have points and no fit for your partner's suit.

Hand D has a fit and no points, and you should jump to 4♠. From your perspective, the opponents can make a slam, and you want to take up as much of their bidding space as you possibly can. Even though your side does not have many points, **your spade fit will prevent your side from getting hurt too badly in 4♠.**

C. Overcalls

There are three purposes of an overcall, which are as follows:

1) Constructive – the hand may belong to your side.
2) Obstructive – your overcall takes up bidding space from the opponents.
3) Lead-directional – you want your partner to lead the suit that you have overcalled.

Of these three reasons, the constructive purpose of an overcall is by far the most important reason.

An overcall at the one-level is a necessarily wide-ranging bid and shows 8 to 17 points. If you are in the lower end of this range, you should have a good suit that you want your partner to lead. You should overcall frequently at the one-level with a good suit – it may be your last chance to enter the auction. You should also play **a new suit response to a one-level overcall as non-forcing**. This enables both partners to make lead-directional bids without getting too high. With a good hand, you can always **cuebid the opponent's suit** to force your partner to bid again.

For example, suppose you hold: ♠ AKQ94
                                  ♥ 53
                                  ♦ 876
                                  ♣ 962

If your RHO opens 1♣, 1♦ or 1♥, you should overcall 1♠ with this hand. Overcalling 1♠ satisfies all three purposes of an overcall.

Here is an example of this overcalling style in action:

DLR: South   ♠ 965
VUL: None   ♥ 8652
Matchpoints   ♦ Q92
                    ♣ K97

♠ AQT43   ♠ 72
♥ Q97   ♥ KJ
♦ 86   ♦ KJT743
♣ T43   ♣ 862

                    ♠ KJ8
                    ♥ AT43
                    ♦ A5
                    ♣ AQJ5

South	West	North	East
1♣	1♠	Pass	2♦
DBL	Pass	3♣	All Pass

Notice that East and West have both been able to enter the auction and indicate their best suit for their partner to lead without getting into any trouble. If you play that a new suit over an overcall is forcing, East would have to pass his partner's 1♠ overcall, as he is not strong enough to make a forcing bid. South would now be able to rebid 1NT to show a balanced hand stronger than a 1NT opening, and he would make at least seven tricks after an opening spade lead. However, on a diamond opening lead, declarer can only take six tricks in a notrump contract.

Partner is entitled to take an inference by your failure to overcall at the one-level. If you could have overcalled a suit at the one-level and failed to do so, partner will tend to lead another suit. For example, if your LHO opens 1♥, your partner passes, and the opponents get to 3NT, the opening leader will tend not to lead a spade, since his partner could have overcalled 1♠ but failed to do so. This inference does not apply to two-level overcalls, since your partner needs an opening bid to overcall a suit at the two-level.

Overcalling in a suit at the two-level without jumping shows

opening bid values or better with a good five-card or longer suit. Of course, the better your suit, the fewer high card points you need to overcall at the two-level. Unlike a one-level overcall, a new suit by an unpassed responding hand is **forcing** for one round, and a cuebid of the opponent's suit shows a limit raise or better in support of the overcaller's suit.

A little creativity never hurts in deciding how to come in over the opponent's opening bid. Here is an example of a creative overcall:

```
DLR: West          ♠ JT872
VUL: Both          ♥ Q62
Matchpoints        ♦ A62
                   ♣ 62

 ♠ 963                          ♠ AKQ
 ♥ T9                           ♥ AJ8743
 ♦ T983                         ♦ QJ74
 ♣ 9754                         ♣ ——

                   ♠ 54
                   ♥ K5
                   ♦ K5
                   ♣ AKQJT83
```

South	West	North	East
	Pass	Pass	1♥
3NT!	All Pass		

With a solid seven-card suit and a likely heart trick behind the opening bidder, South gambled that his partner could provide a ninth trick. This is a very good tactic to use when you have a solid minor suit. Nine tricks are generally easier to take than eleven, and on this hand, 5♣ has no chance while 3NT is laydown.

Is it ever right to overcall on a four-card suit? It is frequently the only action you can take to show values. Over your RHO's 1♦ opening bid, you should overcall on a four-card suit with either of the following hands:

HAND A	HAND B
♠ AKJ8	♠ K8
♥ 963	♥ AQJT
♦ K42	♦ 42
♣ Q63	♣ T8753
Overcall 1♠	Overcall 1♥

In order to overcall on a four-card suit, you must have a reasonably good suit and values, and your hand must be unsuitable for any other action. Both of these hands satisfy all three reasons for making an overcall (see page 25). On Hand A, it is losing tactics to make a takeout double with 4-3-3-3 distribution. Overcalling 1♠ will get partner off to your side's best opening lead and does not preclude other contracts if it is your hand. On Hand B, the fact that you have a five-card club suit is irrelevant – you want your partner to lead a heart, and if it is your hand, you probably want to play it either in hearts or in notrump.

D. Opening Lead Style

A basic principle which you should follow on opening lead is **to lead from a sequence whenever possible.** Leading the king from KQx is a much better lead than leading low from Qxxx, even against a notrump contract. A sequence lead combines safety with aggression and rarely gives up a trick, whereas leading low from Qxxx or Kxxx frequently does cost a trick.

If you do adopt this style of leading from sequences, leading an honor against a notrump contract and then following with the next lower touching honor **asks partner not to unblock** because you have led from a short suit. For example:

HAND A

Opening Leader
KQ5

Partner
A92

HAND B

Opening Leader
KQJ85

Partner
A92

On Hand A, the opening leader starts with the king and continues with the queen, asking his partner not to unblock the ace. On Hand B, the opening leader starts with the king and continues with the jack, showing where his sequence ends and enabling his partner to play the ace and continue the suit.

One principle, which comes from experience, is that if your side preempts and the opponents end up in 3NT, you should believe your opponents. They have a stopper in your suit, and you should consider leading another suit, hoping to put your partner on lead to lead your suit through the declarer. Here is an example hand:

DLR: East
VUL: None
Rubber Bridge

```
                      ♠ KT2
                      ♥ K74
                      ♦ T75
                      ♣ AK54

    ♠ A964                          ♠ Q53
    ♥ A2                            ♥ 98653
    ♦ KJ963                         ♦ 82
    ♣ 86                            ♣ 732

                      ♠ J87
                      ♥ QJT
                      ♦ AQ4
                      ♣ QJT9
```

South	West	North	East
			Pass
1♣	1♦	2♦	Pass
2NT	Pass	3NT	All Pass

North's 2♦ cuebid showed a limit raise or better in clubs, and resulted in N-S getting to 3NT. The fate of this contract depends on the opening lead. South announced that he had diamonds stopped when he bid 2NT, and east did not double north's 2♦ cuebid to get a diamond lead. If west leads a diamond, declarer wins dummy's ten, knocks out the ace of hearts, and leads a spade to dummy's king to make nine tricks. If west is listening to the bidding and leads a spade, declarer can only make eight tricks — east gets in with the queen of spades to lead a diamond through declarer, and the defenders take three spades, one diamond and one heart to defeat the contract.

When dummy will have a long, strong suit, **you need to take your tricks quickly, before dummy's long suit becomes established.** If declarer has bid notrump, showing a stopper in your suit, you must make sure that you knock out that stopper immediately. Here is a hand to illustrate this principle:

DLR: South	♠ J3
VUL: N-S	♥ AK7
Matchpoints	♦ KQJT94
	♣ 42

♠ AQT987	♠ 52
♥ 43	♥ QJT98
♦ A65	♦ 32
♣ 76	♣ JT98

♠ K64
♥ 652
♦ 87
♣ AKQ53

South	West	North	East
1♣	1♠	2♦	Pass
2NT	Pass	3NT	All Pass

When south bid 2NT, he announced that he held the king of spades. West realized that he had to set up his spade suit before declarer set up dummy's diamonds, so he led the **ace** of spades in order to look at the dummy. After this lead, it was easy for west to continue with the queen of spades, pinning the jack in dummy, and declarer had to go down two, losing five spades and a diamond. On the standard lead of the ten of spades, declarer would be able to win the jack in dummy and still have a spade stopper. Declarer would now knock out the ace of diamonds and make eleven tricks for a top score.

KEY POINTS

1. In order to open the bidding, you need at least two quick tricks and a convenient rebid. If your hand meets these requirements, you should open the bidding at the one-level regardless of how many points you have.

2. Tend to open 1♣ in first and second seats with four cards in each minor. In third and fourth seats, open the better minor in order to direct your partner's opening lead should your side defend the hand.

3. Subtract one point when your distribution is 4-3-3-3.

4. There are three purposes of an overcall: a) Constructive; b) Obstructive; and c) Lead Directional. Of these three reasons, the constructive purpose is the most important.

5. An overcall at the one-level shows 8 to 17 points. If you are in the lower end of this range, you must have a good suit in order to make an overcall.

6. A non-jump overcall at the two-level shows opening bid values or better. With a very good suit, this requirement can be shaded down slightly.

7. Do not be afraid to overcall on a good four-card suit at the one-level if no other action is appropriate.

8. A weak two bid should contain a good six-card suit with two of the top three or three of the top five honors, with at most one outside ace or king.

9. When responding to a weak two bid, always raise your partner when you have support for his suit, regardless of how many points you have. Without a fit in partner's suit, you should generally pass.

10. If you lead from an honor sequence against a notrump contract and continue with the next lower touching honor, you are asking partner not to unblock because you have led from a short suit.

11. If you make a preemptive bid and the opponents end up in 3NT, try to lead another suit unless your suit contains a solid honor sequence.

BIDDING QUIZ

1. None vulnerable, you hold:

	RHO	You
♠ AKQ7	1♣	?
♥ 743		
♦ A82		
♣ 632		

2. Both vulnerable, you hold:

♠ A83
♥ K754
♦ AQ7
♣ KQ6   What is your opening bid?

3. Vulnerable versus not, you hold:

	RHO	You
♠ AKT964	1♦	?
♥ AQ9		
♦ 53		
♣ Q7		

4. Non-vulnerable versus vulnerable, you hold:

	RHO	You	LHO	Partner
♠ KQ6	1NT	Pass	3NT	All Pass
♥ T85				
♦ Q973				
♣ 543				

What is your opening lead?

5. Non-vulnerable versus vulnerable, you hold:

	RHO	You	LHO	Partner
♠ KQ6	1NT	Pass	2♣	Pass
♥ T85	2♥	Pass	3NT	All Pass
♦ Q973				
♣ 543		What is your opening lead?		

6. None vulnerable, you hold:

	RHO	You	LHO	Partner
♠ 4	1♣	2♥	DBL	Pass
♥ KJ9753	2NT	Pass	3NT	All Pass
♦ Q972				
♣ 95		What is your opening lead?		

ANSWERS

1. **Overcall 1♠** – This is an example of a hand that should overcall on a good four-card suit. You have values and no other appropriate bid to make.

2. **Open 1NT** – Although you have eighteen points, you should subtract one point for your 4-3-3-3 distribution and treat this as a balanced seventeen-point hand.

3. **Overcall 1♠** – You have a very strong overcall, and you will show your strength by jumping in spades at your next turn. However, you are not strong enough to double first and then bid spades – that sequence shows eighteen or more points.

4. **Lead the king of spades** – This auction screams for a major suit lead, since the opponents made no effort to find a major suit fit via Stayman. Lead the king of spades, and if your partner encourages in spades, continue with the queen of spades to show that you led from a short suit.

5. **Lead the three of diamonds** – Now that the dummy has shown a four-card spade suit, you should make your normal fourth best lead.

6. **Lead the two of diamonds** – Since your partner never supported hearts and the opponents freely bid 3NT over your preemptive bid, there is a good chance that a heart lead will give away a trick. Lead your second suit, and hope that partner has some strength in diamonds.

CHAPTER 2

DISTRIBUTION

A. <u>Distribution Versus High Card Points</u>

Most bridge players count their high card points in order to assess the value of their hands. They open the bidding with thirteen or more points, respond to their partner's opening bid with six or more points, and try to determine whether or not their combined point count is sufficient to make a partscore, a game, or a slam.

This approach works well when both hands are **balanced**. With two balanced hands, the partnership will need approximately 26 points to make a game in notrump or in a major suit, and 33 points to make a small slam. However, when the two hands are **unbalanced**, games and slams can be reached with much less than the normal number of high card points. Here is an extreme contrived example where north-south can make a grand slam in spades on a combined total of five points:

```
                    ♠ T9876
                    ♥ ——
                    ♦ 5432
                    ♣ 5432

    ♠ K                             ♠ Q
    ♥ KQJ                           ♥ AT9
    ♦ AQT8                          ♦ KJ976
    ♣ AQT87                         ♣ KJ96

                    ♠ AJ5432
                    ♥ 8765432
                    ♦ ——
                    ♣ ——
```

Obviously, nobody would actually bid to the seven-level with the North-South hands. However, with the trumps dividing 1-1 and the hearts dividing 3-3, declarer is able to draw trumps in one round and trump three hearts in the dummy to make all thirteen tricks. This hand shows the power of **distribution** – because of the voids in the north and south hands, the opponents could not take a single trick despite holding 35 high card points between them.

Success and failure at the bridge table is measured by **the number of tricks your side takes**, and not by how many points each side happens to hold. Distribution is a very powerful factor in determining the number of tricks that each side can take. The basic principle is to **bid very aggressively when your side has a fit, but be very conservative if the hand looks like a misfit.**

Suppose you hold: ♠ 3
♥ K874
♦ QJ6
♣ A9865

If your partner opens 1♥, it is perfectly acceptable to respond 2♣ with this hand, even if you are playing two over one forcing to game. Your heart fit dramatically increases the trick-taking power of your combined hands, and you want to force to game with this hand even opposite a minimum 1♥ opening bid. Your heart fit increases the possibility that the opponents have a fit also – if both sides have double fits, this hand could be a **double game swing**, where both sides can make a game. You want to make it difficult for the opponents to come into the auction, which is a further advantage of bidding 2♣.

On the other hand, if your partner opens 1♠, the value of your hand decreases because of the misfit, and your only reasonable action is to respond 1NT. Game is unlikely unless partner has extra values, or your side has a fit in hearts or clubs. Over your 1NT response, partner will bid a four-card heart or club suit if he has one.

Suppose you hold: ♠ Q98
                       ♥ AQ652
                       ♦ 5
                       ♣ J754

Your LHO opens 1♠, your partner overcalls 2♦, and your RHO passes. **Do not bid 2♥ with this hand** – your bid is forcing, and if your partner does not fit hearts, he will probably rebid 3♦, which the opponents might double. It is true that your side might have a heart fit, but you cannot risk looking for it on a potential misfit hand. You should just pass and hope for the best. Generally, on misfit hands, **stop bidding as soon as possible.** You may not be in the best contract, but attempting to improve the contract can often lead to disaster when no fit exists.

With this same hand, if your partner overcalls 2♣ instead of 2♦, you would be happy to bid 2♥ as a forcing bid. If your partner fits hearts, you may have a game, and if your partner does not fit hearts, he can always return to clubs, where your side has a minimum nine-card fit.

The way to show your partner that you have a fit in his suit is to follow the principle of **Support with Support.** When your partner opens the bidding, either at the one-level or with a preemptive two-bid or three-bid, **the most important feature you can show your partner is that you have support for his opening bid suit.** The most important rule of bidding is to SUPPORT partner with SUPPORT in the trump suit.

Here are some examples of **Support with Support:**

You Hold	You	LHO	Partner	RHO
♠ K643	1♣	Pass	1♠	3♥
♥ 64	?			
♦ A75				
♣ AQ96				

Bid 3♠ – Although you would only bid 2♠ without competition, you must stretch to show a fit in a competitive auction. It is okay to bid one level higher in a competitive auction than you normally would in order to show a fit in your partner's suit.

You Hold	You	LHO	Partner	RHO
♠ K643	1♣	Pass	1♠	3♥
♥ K74	?			
♦ K8				
♣ AKQ5				

Bid 4♠ – When you would have had a normal 3♠ bid in a noncompetitive auction, you have to jump to 4♠ with this type of hand, in order to differentiate it from the first hand above.

You Hold	Partner	RHO	You	LHO
♠ QT864	1♠	2♦	?	
♥ 86				
♦ 64				
♣ KJT7				

Jump to 3♠ or 4♠, depending on vulnerability – You want to preempt as high as possible with a weak hand and a fit and make your opponents guess what to do at a high level.

You Hold	You	LHO	Partner	RHO
♠ 853	1♣	1♦	1♥	1♠
♥ AQ76	?			
♦ KT				
♣ KJ85				

Bid 2♥ – Although you have a minimum opening hand which got worse when your LHO bid diamonds, **you must bid 2♥ to show the fit.**

You Hold	Partner	RHO	You	LHO
♠ 974	1♥	2♦	?	
♥ K974				
♦ 74				
♣ JT83				

Jump to **3♥**, preemptive – If your RHO had passed, you might also have passed, as bidding on such a weak hand would tend to get your side too high when your partner held a good hand. Once RHO overcalls, however, **you must jam the auction as high as possible and make the opponents guess what to do at a high level.** Remember that if you had a good hand and support for your partner's suit, you would cuebid 3D, the opponent's suit. This cuebid says nothing about your diamond holding – you are showing your partner a limit raise or better in hearts. Since all good hands with heart support would cuebid the opponent's suit, this frees the jump to 3H to show a weak hand with four-card or longer heart support.

Here is an example of **Support with Support** in the context of an entire hand:

DLR: East   ♠ 9542
VUL: Both   ♥ KJ74
Matchpoints   ♦ T73
             ♣ K7

   ♠ Q6   ♠ K3
   ♥ QT   ♥ 853
   ♦ Q9652   ♦ AKJ84
   ♣ Q854   ♣ AJ2

          ♠ AJT87
          ♥ A962
          ♦ ——
          ♣ T963

South	West	North	East
			1NT
2 ♠	2NT	3 ♠	Pass
Pass	DBL	All Pass	

North did not have many high card points, but he knew that his side had at least nine spades, so he competed to 3♠ over west's natural 2NT bid. West, with eight points opposite a strong notrump opening, made a penalty double of 3♠, but, with spades dividing 2-2, **he was unable to prevent declarer from making an overtrick.** This hand is an illustration of the fact that **points do not take tricks – fits and long suits are what matter** when the opponents are bidding on distributional values.

When you have a fit in your partner's suit, do not hesitate to support that suit, even with very few high card points. Here is another example of bidding with a fit in your partner's suit:

DLR: West
VUL: Both
Rubber Bridge

	♠ ——	
	♥ 7543	
	♦ QT963	
	♣ Q942	

♠ AQ43	♠ KJ876
♥ AKQ86	♥ T92
♦ 5	♦ 74
♣ T87	♣ K53

♠ T952
♥ J
♦ AKJ82
♣ AJ6

South	West	North	East
	1♥	Pass	1♠
2♦	3♠	5♦!	Pass
Pass	DBL	All Pass	

Although north had a very weak hand, **he had a big fit in his partner's suit**, so he jumped to 5♦. With clubs breaking 3-3, this game turned out to be cold with a combined seventeen points between the two hands. Notice that E-W can make a game their way in spades - in fact, south must underlead his ace-king of diamonds at trick one in order to defeat 5♠! On the ace of diamonds lead, declarer can ruff a diamond in dummy, draw trumps, and throw two clubs away on the good hearts to make eleven tricks. This is an example of a **double game swing**, where both sides can make a game.

How high should you raise your partner's suit when you have a fit? A good guideline to follow is to **compete to the level that corresponds to your side's total number of trumps**. For example, with nine combined trumps, bid to the three-level, and with ten combined trumps, compete to the four-level. This guideline is known as **The Law of Total Trumps.**

Notice that no mention was made of how many points you need to raise your partner's suit. When you have a fit in your partner's suit, forget about points and bid to the level of your side's total trumps. The **Law of Total Trumps** will protect you. If you compete to 4♠ with a ten-card spade fit, and the opponents double you and beat you three tricks, they could have made at least a game, and possibly a slam, in their own long suit. The operating rule for raising your partner in these situations is: **Don't count points, count trumps!**

Suppose you hold either of the following hands:

HAND A	HAND B
♠ AT65	♠ 9832
♥ A3	♥ 765
♦ KQT74	♦ Q9742
♣ KJ	♣ 5

If your partner opens the bidding with 2♠, **you should jump to 4♠ with each of these hands.** On Hand A, you are bidding to make your game; on Hand B, you are taking an advanced sacrifice, knowing that it is the opponents' hand. When you have a weak hand with a fit for your partner's long suit, **compete to the level of your total trumps immediately and let the opponents guess what to do at a high level.**

Conversely, when you do not fit your partner's suit, you should bid very conservatively, regardless of how many points you have. Remember that points do not take tricks — trumps and long suits are what take tricks at bridge. The corollary of Support with Support is that when there is a misfit, **stop bidding.**

Here are some examples of bidding with a misfit:

Opener	Responder	Opener	Responder
♠ ——	♠ AQJ9763	1♦	1♠
♥ QJ7	♥ T5	3♣ (game force)	3♠
♦ AQJ87	♦ T6	4♣	4♠
♣ AKJ73	♣ 85		

On this hand, responder will need to be very lucky to make 4♠. He will need either 3-3 spades, or 4-2 spades with the ten falling doubleton, and also the diamond king onside to make his contract.

There is nothing wrong with the bidding on this hand. The opener has a hand that wants to force to game opposite a response, and the responder certainly has a rebiddable suit. This hand illustrates how difficult it is to make a game when the hands do not fit well.

Opener	Responder	Opener	Responder
♠ 9	♠ KT542	3♥	Pass
♥ AKJ7654	♥ ——		
♦ 76	♦ AKT5		
♣ T62	♣ KQ85		

Once again, the opener will need moderate luck just to make 3♥. Although the responder has a good hand, it is no longer a good hand when his partner opens with a 3♥ preempt!

Here is an example of a misfit in the context of an entire hand:

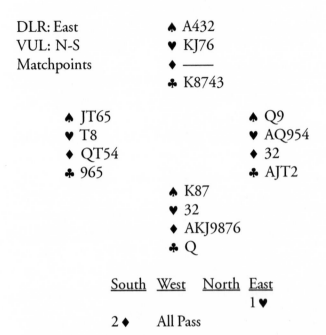

DLR: East   ♠ A432
VUL: N-S   ♥ KJ76
Matchpoints   ♦ ——
            ♣ K8743

♠ JT65   ♠ Q9
♥ T8   ♥ AQ954
♦ QT54   ♦ 32
♣ 965   ♣ AJT2

           ♠ K87
           ♥ 32
           ♦ AKJ9876
           ♣ Q

South	West	North	East
			1♥
2♦	All Pass		

Despite holding eleven points, north realized the hand was a misfit and passed. The KJ of hearts in front of the heart bidder and the void in his partner's suit made game very unlikely. On this hand, N-S have a combined total of twenty-four points and have to struggle just to make 2♦. Making 2♦ was a top score for N-S on this hand; those norths that bid with a misfit got too high and were frequently doubled.

When you have a very distributional hand, your hand is generally an **offensive hand** — this means that your hand will take a lot of tricks if your long suit is trumps, but you may not take many tricks on defense. For example, here is an offensive hand:

♠ KQJT965
♥ 4
♦ QJ8
♣ 63

With spades as trumps, your hand is worth 6½ tricks, and you should open this hand 3♠ even if you are vulnerable. On defense, your hand will take very few tricks.

When you have a hand that can take tricks either on offense or defense, you have a hand with **transferable values** - your hand will take tricks either declaring or defending. Here is an example of a hand with transferable values:

♠ AQ86
♥ K97
♦ KJ54
♣ K4

This hand is valuable either on offense or on defense – a typical 1NT opening.

When you have a hand that will take slow tricks on defense but contains very few quick tricks, you have a **defensive hand**. Here is an example:

♠ QJT9
♥ QJ6
♦ KJ76
♣ QJ

This hand adds up to 13 points, but you should pass if you are the dealer. You have very little offensive potential.

When you have a distributional hand, you should make a vigorous effort to declare the hand, since these hands will take a lot of tricks on offense but very few tricks if your side winds up defending. Grant Baze, one of America's leading bridge players, says, "6-5, Come Alive" – when you are dealt a two-suited hand, you have to compete vigorously to declare the hand. One of the worst things that can happen to you at any form of bridge, but particularly when playing Rubber Bridge or Swiss Teams, is a **double game swing**. For this reason, when you have a distributional hand, your thinking should be, "When in doubt, bid one more". Particularly when you have support for your partner's suit, you should **show the fit first** before doubling the opponents for penalty. Here is an example which illustrates this point:

```
DLR: South          ♠ AKT4
VUL: Both           ♥ 9763
Matchpoints         ♦ ——
                    ♣ KQ864

    ♠ 2                             ♠ J73
    ♥ QJ82                          ♥ K4
    ♦ AKQJ95                        ♦ 8763
    ♣ 72                            ♣ AT53

                    ♠ Q9865
                    ♥ AT5
                    ♦ T42
                    ♣ J9
```

South	West	North	East
Pass	1♦	DBL	1NT
2♠	3♦	4♠	DBL
Pass	Pass	Pass	

West opened the bidding and freely rebid 3♦, so when N-S bid 4♠, east doubled indignantly, knowing that his side held the majority of the points. While it is true that E-W had most of the points, **4♠ was unbeatable on this hand**. In fact, declarer frequently made an overtrick when the defenders failed to switch to hearts early in the hand, and no declarer made less than ten tricks! Note that E-W have an excellent save in 5♦ doubled, which only goes down one.

Here is another "high card point" double:

```
DLR: East          ♠ ——
VUL: Both          ♥ K963
Swiss Teams        ♦ A82
                   ♣ AT9752

   ♠ KQ32                        ♠ T75
   ♥ 2                           ♥ A84
   ♦ KJT96                       ♦ Q543
   ♣ K64                         ♣ QJ8

                   ♠ AJ9864
                   ♥ QJT75
                   ♦ 7
                   ♣ 3
```

South	West	North	East
			Pass
Pass	1♦	2♣	2♦
2♠	Pass	3♣	Pass
3♥	Pass	4♥	DBL
All Pass			

East's double is the kind of error that is made all the time. This type of double is known as a "point counter's double". A point counter doubles because he knows that his side holds most of the points. Of course, the opponents are bidding on distributional values and frequently make their doubled contract, sometimes with overtricks. The dedicated point counter will just mutter "unlucky" and make the same kind of losing double the next time around. But are these doubles really unlucky? No, they are losing tactics and show a lack of realization that the opponents are bidding on good distributional values. On this particular hand, with clubs dividing 3-3, 4♥ doubled makes no fewer than twelve tricks! Remember that when the opponents are bidding at a high level and your side has the majority of the points, the opponents must have compensating distribution to compete to such a high level.

The following hand is a good example of aggressive bidding with a weak distributional hand and a fit:

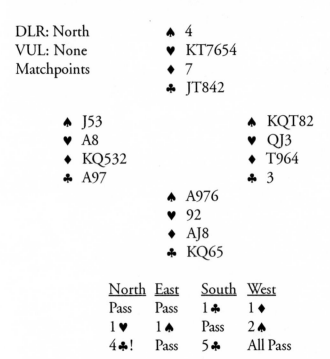

DLR: North
VUL: None
Matchpoints

♠ 4
♥ KT7654
♦ 7
♣ JT842

♠ J53
♥ A8
♦ KQ532
♣ A97

♠ KQT82
♥ QJ3
♦ T964
♣ 3

♠ A976
♥ 92
♦ AJ8
♣ KQ65

North	East	South	West
Pass	Pass	1♣	1♦
1♥	1♠	Pass	2♠
4♣!	Pass	5♣	All Pass

Although north had a weak hand, the fact that he had a club fit with his partner enabled him to bid the hand aggressively once he had passed initially. With the ace of hearts onside, declarer only lost one heart and one club to make his eighteen-point game.

When you have a two-suited hand, you should be willing to compete and show both of your suits. Here is another example of "6-5, Come Alive":

```
DLR: East           ♠ 4
VUL: Both           ♥ J6
Matchpoints         ♦ J43
                    ♣ J987642
```

```
    ♠ Q87                       ♠ KJ2
    ♥ 753                       ♥ Q98
    ♦ KQ865                     ♦ AT97
    ♣ KQ                        ♣ AT3
```

```
                    ♠ AT9653
                    ♥ AKT42
                    ♦ 2
                    ♣ 5
```

South	West	North	East
			1♦
1♠	2♠	Pass	2NT
3♥	Pass	Pass	DBL
All Pass			

West cuebid 2♠ at his first turn to show a limit raise or better in diamonds. East rebid 2NT, and south competed again by bidding his heart suit. When this came back to east, he chose the losing bid of double. The defenders led two rounds of diamonds, and declarer ruffed the second round in his hand. Declarer played the ace of spades and **ruffed a spade with dummy's jack of hearts.** Declarer now played a heart to the ten, drew trumps with the ace and the king, and gave up a spade trick. With both major suits breaking 3-3 and the queen of hearts onside, declarer made a doubled overtrick for +930. **Notice that east-west are cold for 3NT on this hand!**

B. Two-Suited Hands

There are two bids that are commonly used to show two-suited hands – Michaels and the Unusual Notrump. The advantage of

these bids is that if partner fits one of your suits, you can successfully compete in that suit, possibly making a game on very few
points or finding a successful sacrifice against the opponents' game.
The disadvantage of these two-suited bids is that if the opponents
wind up playing the hand, you have drawn a roadmap of your
distribution for the declarer, and he will be able to play the hand
very well.

Since making a two-suited bid gives away valuable distributional information to your opponents, you must have a real chance
of playing the contract if you find a fit with your partner. Therefore, the texture of your suits must be good – there is a big difference between QJT95 and Q8732, particularly if partner had to
take a preference on a two-card suit! Suit texture is much more
important than high card points in determining whether or not to
make a two-suited bid.

Generally, the point requirements for these two-suited bids
are either less than an opening bid or a very strong playing hand.
With a strong hand, you will make another bid to show the stronger range. Hands in the 12–16 point range are generally overcalled in the higher-ranking suit, hoping to bid the other suit later
if the auction permits.

When your partner makes a two-suited bid, you must evaluate your hand in terms of **the high cards you possess in those two
suits**. Points in your partner's two suits are worth their weight in
gold, whereas points in the other two suits will be virtually worth-
less. What would you bid with each of the following hands after
your LHO opens 1♥, your partner jumps to 2NT, and your RHO
competes to 3♥?

HAND A	HAND B	HAND C
♠ 8762	♠ KQJ65	♠ 987643
♥ Q82	♥ KJ64	♥ 86
♦ KT62	♦ 85	♦ A5
♣ A7	♣ 73	♣ K92

With Hand A, your hand is enormous when partner shows both minor suits, and you should jump directly to 5♦. With Hand B, you should pass over your RHO's 3♥ bid. With all of your points in the major suits, your hand will be quite useless opposite partner's minor two-suiter. Some players would prefer to double 3♥ for penalties, but your heart holding is finesseable, since you are sitting in front of the 1♥ opener. With Hand C, you again have a great hand for your partner, with all of your points in the minor suits, and you should jump to 5♣!

When you have a strong hand, do not be afraid to bid out your shape. Bidding out your shape means starting out by bidding your long suit, and continuing to bid your second suit when the opponents compete further, and is vastly superior to making an off-shape takeout double. Here is an example:

DLR: West
VUL: None
Rubber Bridge

```
                        ♠ QJT
                        ♥ T53
                        ♦ J875
                        ♣ K97

        ♠ 72                        ♠ 8653
        ♥ KJ4                       ♥ AQ982
        ♦ Q962                      ♦ KT3
        ♣ T652                      ♣ 8

                        ♠ AK94
                        ♥ 76
                        ♦ A4
                        ♣ AQJ43
```

South	West	North	East
	Pass	Pass	1♥
2♣	2♥	Pass	Pass
2♠	Pass	3♠	Pass
4♠	All Pass		

When east opened light with a 1♥ bid in third seat, south could not make a takeout double with a doubleton diamond, so he bid 2♣. When the auction got back to him, he was strong enough to reverse into 2♠. North raised spades, and N-S got to their best game contract. After two rounds of hearts, declarer was able to trump the third heart in dummy, draw trumps and claim eleven tricks.

Here is another example of bidding out your distribution:

DLR: East	♠ J652
VUL: Both	♥ K2
Swiss Teams	♦ 95
	♣ Q9652

♠ 743	♠ Q
♥ AT98	♥ QJ7643
♦ Q3	♦ A62
♣ KT87	♣ AJ4

	♠ AKT98
	♥ 5
	♦ KJT874
	♣ 3

South	West	North	East
			1♥
2♦	3♦	Pass	4♥
4♠	Pass	Pass	DBL
All Pass			

Rather than make an off-shape takeout double, south simply bid out his distribution, overcalling in diamonds at the two-level and then bidding spades at the four-level. East thought he was in a forcing pass situation, so he doubled 4♠, but the contract could not be defeated on the lie of the cards. West started with the ace of hearts and shifted to a club to partner's jack. Declarer ruffed the club continuation, and played three rounds of trumps, ending in dummy. Declarer led a diamond from dummy, and when east played low, declarer won his king. Declarer gave up a diamond and ruffed a diamond with dummy's last trump, setting up the diamond suit, and claimed ten tricks.

Here is one final example of bidding out your shape:

```
DLR: East          ♠ 7653
VUL: Both          ♥ K7
Swiss Teams        ♦ T93
                   ♣ QJT9

    ♠ J82                      ♠ AQT4
    ♥ T83                      ♥ QJ4
    ♦ QJ8764                   ♦ AK52
    ♣ 4                        ♣ 85

                   ♠ K9
                   ♥ A9652
                   ♦ ——
                   ♣ AK7632
```

South	West	North	East
			1NT
2♣	2♦	3♣	3♦
3♥	Pass	5♣	All Pass

Despite east opening the bidding with a strong notrump, N-S can make no fewer than twelve tricks in clubs.

KEY POINTS

1. Bid aggressively when you have a fit with your partner's suit, but be conservative when you do not have a fit.

2. When you have a fit with your partner's suit, Support with Support, regardless of how many points you have.

3. In a competitive auction, compete to the level of your side's total number of trumps, regardless of how many points you have. Don't count points, count trumps!

4. When you have support for your partner's suit, show the fit first rather than double the opponents. When in doubt, bid one more and avoid an adverse double game swing.

5. With 6-5 distribution, you should be inclined to bid your suits. 6-5, Come Alive!

6. When you make a two-suited bid, you ought to have good texture in your suits.

7. When your partner makes a two-suited bid, you should evaluate your hand in terms of your holdings in partner's suits.

8. Bidding out your distribution with a strong hand is vastly superior to making an off-shape takeout double.

BIDDING QUIZ

1. None vulnerable, you hold:

	LHO	Partner	RHO	You
♠ JT9863	1♣	3♥	Pass	?
♥ Q943				
♦ J				
♣ A2				

2. Both vulnerable, you hold:

	Partner	RHO	You
♠ ——	1♣	1♠	?
♥ T9			
♦ AJT754			
♣ Q9863			

3. Vulnerable vs. not, you hold:

	You	LHO	Partner	RHO
♠ ——	Pass	Pass	1♠	Pass
♥ AT6543	2♥	Pass	2♠	Pass
♦ 97	?			
♣ KQ765				

4. Non-vulnerable vs. vulnerable, you hold:

	You	LHO	Partner	RHO
♠ AK94	1♣	Pass	1♥	2♠
♥ A854	?			
♦ 8				
♣ J972				

5. Both vulnerable, you hold:

	You	LHO	Partner	RHO
♠ QT942	Pass	1♦	2♦	DBL
♥ 5	?			
♦ J764				
♣ A83				

6. None vulnerable, you hold:

	You	LHO	Partner	RHO
♠ 8654	You	LHO	Partner	RHO
♥ T865	Pass	Pass	2♠	3♥
♦ 653	?			
♣ K9				

ANSWERS

1. **Bid 5♥** – Compete to the level of your total trumps immediately. Your partner has seven trumps and you have four-card support, so jump to 5♥ and let the opponents guess what to do at the five-level.

2. **Bid 2♦** – Since you have a big fit in clubs, you can bid aggressively with your hand. You intend to bid 5♣ if your opponents compete to 4♠.

3. **Bid 3♣** – Since you are a passed hand, your bid is not forcing. You are bidding out your shape and telling your partner that you must play in one of your long suits. Remember, 6-5, come alive!

4. **Bid 3♥** – When you have support for your partner's suit, show the support first; double the opponents only after you have supported your partner's suit.

5. **Jump to 4♠** – This follows the Law of Total Trumps – your side has a ten-card spade fit, so jump to the level of your total trumps immediately.

6. **Jump to 4♠** – Your side has a ten-card spade fit. Jump to the level of your total trumps, and let the opponents guess what to do at the five-level.

CHAPTER 3

BIDDING PRINCIPLES YOUR MOTHER NEVER TAUGHT YOU

A. <u>Raising Partner's Major Suit with Three-Card Support</u>*

Suppose you open the bidding at the one-level and partner responds in a major suit. When should you raise your partner's major with three-card support? The first requirement is that you must have shortness (two or fewer cards) in an unbid suit. The time that it is desirable to play in a 4-3 fit is **when you can ruff in the short trump hand.** With a doubleton in an unbid suit, use the following guideline: If the doubleton is Qx or better, rebid 1NT, but if the doubleton is Jx or worse, consider raising partner's major with three-card support. Generally, the three-card support should include an honor. You do not have to raise your partner's major suit with three-card support and a small doubleton. For example, if your hand is:

♠ 754
♥ J5
♦ KQ4
♣ AQJ86

Rebid 1NT rather than 2♠ with three small spades.

* These concepts are adopted from Marshall Miles' excellent book, "Stronger Competitive Bidding".

If you have a singleton or a void in an unbid suit, **you should always raise your partner's major suit** with three-card support.

The second requirement to raise partner's major suit with three-card support is that you have a minimum opening bid. With extra values, bid another suit first and then raise partner's major. Note that bidding another suit and then raising partner's major **always shows extra values**. This is how the opener can show three-card support with extra values and shortness in the unbid suit.

Suppose you hold: ♠ 95
                      ♥ KQ8
                      ♦ AQ954
                      ♣ K96

You open 1♦ and your partner responds 1♥. In Standard American bidding, opener is expected to rebid 1NT rather than raise his partner with only three trumps. The explanation is that although 1NT may be a bad contract, if the opener's partner is strong enough to bid again, the opener can subsequently show good three-card support. Let us look at the flaws in this reasoning:

1) The failure to raise hearts may prevent the opener's side from reaching game. After a raise to 2♥, responder might well bid again with:

HAND A	HAND B
♠ 762	♠ 762
♥ AT953	♥ AT542
♦ KJ9	♦ JT3
♣ QT	♣ AT

With either of these hands, the responder would be encouraged by the double fit, while he would certainly pass after a 1NT rebid.

2) The hand may belong in 4♥ with a 4-3 trump fit if responder holds:

> ♠ 762
> ♥ AJT6
> ♦ KT3
> ♣ A95

It would never occur to the responder that he should look for a heart contract after a 1NT rebid.

3) Failure to raise hearts will lead to a vastly inferior partscore contract when the responder has a five-card heart suit and not enough strength to bid again.

Now that you are convinced that you should raise your partner's major suit immediately with three-card support and ruffing values, how does this change the responder's bidding? There are two changes that the responder should make in his bidding, which are as follows:

1) The responder should no longer bid his four-card majors "up the line". Since the opener is allowed to raise on three-card support, **the responder should strain to bid good four-card suits where he doesn't mind playing in a 4-3 fit.** For example, your partner opens 1♦ and you hold:

HAND A	HAND B
♠ AK97	♠ AKT5
♥ 9532	♥ 9532
♦ J43	♦ 82
♣ 87	♣ Q75

With both of these hands, your response should be 1♠ rather than 1♥. Even if your side has a 4-4 heart fit, you won't have a game in hearts unless partner is strong enough to reverse or to bid 2NT (and in that case you may belong in 3NT despite the heart fit). You might miss a superior partscore contract when partner has four hearts, but you might also reach an inferior partscore contract when partner raises your hearts on three-card support. For example, if partner holds ♠QJ8 ♥QJ8 ♦AKT75 ♣92, partner will raise whichever major you bid to the two-level. I think it is safe to say that you would prefer to play in a 4-3 fit in your strong spade suit rather than your anemic heart suit.

2) If the responder has game-forcing or invitational values with a balanced hand, he should jump to 3NT with a game-forcing hand and bid 2NT with an invitational hand if his major suit length is only 4 cards. This enables the partnership to play in notrump instead of a 4-3 fit when the opener has raised with three-card support. For example, suppose you hold either of the following hands:

HAND A	HAND B
♠ Q97	♠ AJ74
♥ AK83	♥ Q832
♦ J4	♦ 95
♣ AT65	♣ AQ6

Your partner opens 1♦, you respond 1♥, and your partner raises you to 2♥. You should jump to 3NT with each of these hands to give your partner a choice of games. If your partner has four-card support, he will go back to 4♥, but he will pass your 3NT rebid with just three-card support.

Let us take a look at an example of raising with three-card support:

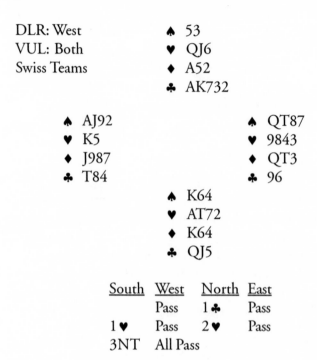

DLR: West		♠ 53	
VUL: Both		♥ QJ6	
Swiss Teams		♦ A52	
		♣ AK732	

♠ AJ92   ♠ QT87
♥ K5   ♥ 9843
♦ J987   ♦ QT3
♣ T84   ♣ 96

♠ K64
♥ AT72
♦ K64
♣ QJ5

South	West	North	East
	Pass	1♣	Pass
1♥	Pass	2♥	Pass
3NT	All Pass		

Notice that either 4♥ or 3NT played by south is cold. In 3NT, if the defenders lead a spade, this gives declarer the ninth trick immediately. Notice that if north rebids 1NT over his partner's 1♥ response, the notrump game will be declared from the wrong side. East will lead the seven of spades, and if declarer plays low, west should apply the **Rule of Eleven** and realize that declarer cannot beat the seven spot. If west properly plays the two of spades on the opening lead, leaving his partner on lead to continue spades, the defenders will collect four spade tricks and eventually win the king of hearts for down one!

Here is another example of this bidding style:

```
DLR: North          ♠ A97
VUL: N-S            ♥ AJ84
Rubber Bridge       ♦ KQ982
                    ♣ 8

    ♠ T652                      ♠ J4
    ♥ Q953                      ♥ T72
    ♦ AT6                       ♦ 74
    ♣ K2                        ♣ JT9643

                    ♠ KQ83
                    ♥ K6
                    ♦ J53
                    ♣ AQ75
```

North	East	South	West
1♦	Pass	1♠	Pass
2♠	Pass	3NT	All Pass

If you play this style of raising with three-card trump support, the responding hand **should always jump to 3NT with an opening bid, stoppers in the unbid suits and only four trumps.** The opener will return to the major suit with four-card support, and will pass 3NT if he raised with just three-card support. On this particular hand, eleven tricks can be made in either spades or notrump, with the heart queen onside and diamonds breaking 3-2.

If you adopt this strategy of raising with three-card support, you will frequently be playing in a 4-3 fit. The strategy of playing in a 4-3 fit is different from that of playing in an eight-card or longer trump fit, and will be discussed in further detail in Chapter 6.

B. <u>Responding Light</u>

When you first learned the rules of bridge, you were taught that the responder needs at least six points in order to respond to his partner's opening bid. This is very good advice for beginners, who need to have everything explained to them in terms of points because they have not yet developed bidding judgment.

As you develop experience at bridge, you learn that it is frequently correct to respond to your partner's opening bid with fewer than six points. There are two instances where it may be right for you to respond with fewer than six points: 1) You have an ace; 2) You have two or fewer cards in your partner's *minor* suit.

If you have an ace, you should respond to your partner's opening bid. Aces are undervalued in the standard point count. An ace is worth more than four points – it is a first round control, and it is a certain entry to one's hand. By responding when you have an ace, you make it difficult for the opponents to get into the bidding. Sometimes you can even steal away a game from the opponents by responding light. Since we intend to pass at our next turn, we won't get too high if our partner has a good hand.

Another reason you should respond to your partner's opening bid of 1♣ or 1♦ with fewer than six points is because you have shortness (two or fewer cards) in your partner's minor suit. By passing, **you are allowing the opponents to control your fate.** When the bidding goes 1♣-P-P, the fourth hand controls the auction. If playing in 1♣ is bad for your side, then the fourth hand will pass and let your partner struggle in a possible 3-1 or 4-1 fit. If it is right for the opponents to compete, it is very easy to balance over 1♣-P-P. Since it is generally not a good idea for the opponents to determine your fate, you should respond with less than six points when your partner opens 1♣ or 1♦ and you have shortness in that suit – make life difficult for your opponents, not your partner!

Here is a spectacular example of responding light:

DLR: South
VUL: Both
Swiss Teams

♠ AKQT
♥ KT3
♦ KQ
♣ Q983

♠ J3
♥ J987
♦ A74
♣ K654

♠ 64
♥ A652
♦ J3
♣ AJT72

♠ 98752
♥ Q4
♦ T98652
♣ —

South	West	North	East
Pass	Pass	1♣	Pass
1♠	Pass	4♠	Pass
Pass	Pass		

With a void in his partner's minor suit, south elected to re-spond 1♠. The opener jumped to 4♠, which made eleven tricks, losing one heart and one diamond. Those south players who passed their partner's 1♣ opening bid **went minus at the one-level** – although north-south can make eleven tricks in spades, they could not make seven tricks in clubs!

C. Modern Preempts

Although I recommend sound weak two opening bids, you still have to take advantage of favorable vulnerability. When you are at favorable vulnerability, you can make very light three-level preemptive openings – you may have only a six-card suit, and your suit quality may be poor. Remember that when the vulnerability is favorable, you can afford to go down three tricks doubled and still get a good score if the opponents can make a vulnerable game.

I recommend hyperlight three-level preempts at favorable vulnerability, especially in first and third seats. Your objective, especially in third seat when your partner is a passed hand, is to get in the opponent's way and make it difficult for them to get to their best spot. Here are some examples of hands that could preempt at the three-level:

HAND 1	HAND 2	HAND 3
♠ QT9862	♠ 3	♠ 4
♥ 4	♥ 52	♥ QJT863
♦ QJ94	♦ T862	♦ J9854
♣ 64	♣ KQT984	♣ 2
Open 3♠	Open 3♣	Open 3♥

All three of these hands have very good distribution, which will protect you from getting hurt badly at the three-level. Remember that when you have an offensive hand, you want to try to become the declarer.

Here is an example of a hyperlight preempt in action:

DLR: South   ♠ 5
VUL: E-W   ♥ AQT54
Matchpoints   ♦ AK752
                  ♣ KQ

♠ A   ♠ K9742
♥ KJ9832   ♥ 6
♦ 76   ♦ QJ93
♣ AJT7   ♣ 652

            ♠ QJT863
            ♥ 7
            ♦ T5
            ♣ 9843

South	West	North	East
3 ♠!	4 ♥	DBL	All Pass

The hyperlight 3♠ opening bid resulted in N-S collecting +1100 against 4♥ doubled.

D. When in Doubt, Bid 3NT

In a competitive auction, you should lean towards bidding 3NT **whenever you have length and slow stoppers in the opponent's suit.** Your length in the opponent's suit, which is a liability when declaring a suit contract, turns into an asset when your side is declaring 3NT. Here is an example of this principle at work:

```
DLR: East            ♠ A
VUL: None            ♥ 85
Matchpoints          ♦ AQJ654
                     ♣ AQ54

      ♠ J93                          ♠ Q652
      ♥ 9                            ♥ AQT64
      ♦ T987                         ♦ 3
      ♣ KT963                        ♣ J72

                     ♠ KT874
                     ♥ KJ732
                     ♦ K2
                     ♣ 8
```

South	West	North	East
			Pass
Pass	Pass	1♦	1♥
1♠	Pass	3♦	Pass
3NT	All Pass		

When north jump rebid 3♦, south followed the principle of bidding 3NT with length and strength in the opponent's suit despite the singleton club. West got off to the best lead of a club, and declarer finessed the queen successfully. A low heart was played to the jack, and declarer returned to dummy with the ace of spades to play another heart. East rose with the ace to return another club, but declarer had twelve tricks for a top score.

E. Opening 1NT With a Five-Card Major

It is generally a good idea to describe your hand in one bid if you can. Therefore, it is perfectly acceptable to open 1NT with a five-card major in order to avoid a subsequent rebid problem. For example, you hold:

♠ Q74　　♥ KQ864　　♦ AQ5　　♣ K7

If you open this hand 1♥ and your partner responds 1♠, what is your rebid? You have an impossible rebid problem – you can no longer describe a balanced hand of 15 to 17 points. Opening 1NT solves all of your problems on this hand.

However, if you have a maximum notrump opening and a five-card major, **this hand is too strong for a 1NT opening**. Opening 1NT with 17 points and a five-card major can easily result in missing a game. Furthermore, you have no rebid problem with seventeen points - if partner responds one notrump, you can raise to two notrump, showing better than a notrump opening. For this reason, when you have a balanced hand and a five-card major suit, you should open 1♥ or 1♠ with seventeen high card points and open 1NT with fifteen or sixteen points.

Here is a hand that took place in a Swiss Teams match:

Opener	Responder
♠ KQ863	♠ JT9
♥ K85	♥ 32
♦ AJ9	♦ KQ875
♣ A6	♣ 943

At one table, the opener bid 1NT, which ended the auction. The opponents led a heart, and declarer knocked out the ace of spades. The opponents were able to cash four heart tricks, and declarer claimed the balance of the tricks for +120.

At the other table, the opener bid 1♠, partner raised to 2♠, and the opener bid 4♠. With spades 3-2, declarer was able to draw trumps and pitch two heart losers away on dummy's good diamonds, making his contract for +620 and an eleven IMP swing.

KEY POINTS

1. As the opener, do not be afraid to raise your partner's major suit response with three-card support when you have shortness in an unbid suit.

2. As the responder, do not jump to game in a major suit if your partner raises your major suit to the two-level if you have only four trumps. Jump to 3NT to offer your partner a choice of games in case your partner raised you with three-card support.

3. As the responder, do not bid your major suits "up the line" when your partner will raise you with three-card support. With a good four-card spade suit and a poor four-card heart suit, it may be right to respond 1♠ to partner's opening bid of 1♣ or 1♦.

4. You should respond to your partner's opening bid with fewer than six points if you have an ace, or if you have shortness (two or fewer cards) in partner's minor suit.

5. At favorable vulnerability, you should preempt at the three-level with very weak hands, especially in first and third seats.

6. Whenever you have length and slow stoppers in the opponent's suit, you should lean in favor of bidding notrump. Your length in the opponent's suit, which is a liability in a suit contract, becomes an asset when you play the hand in notrump.

7. With a balanced hand and a five-card major suit, open 1NT with fifteen or sixteen points, but open the major suit with seventeen points.

BIDDING QUIZ

1. None vulnerable, you hold:

	You	LHO	Partner	RHO
♠ K97	1♣	Pass	1♠	Pass
♥ AQ86	?			
♦ 42				
♣ KJ95				

2. Both vulnerable, you hold:

	Partner	RHO	You
♠ AQT7	1♦	Pass	?
♥ 9754			
♦ K43			
♣ 62			

3. Non-vulnerable versus vulnerable, you hold:

♠ 7
♥ QT97653
♦ K95
♣ 42

What action do you take in first seat?

4. Vulnerable versus non-vulnerable, you hold:

	Partner	RHO	You
♠ 98654	1♣	Pass	?
♥ 743			
♦ KJ6			
♣ 3			

5. None vulnerable, you hold:

	Partner	RHO	You	LHO
♠ AQ86	1♦	Pass	1♠	Pass
♥ K83	2♠	Pass	?	
♦ T7				
♣ KJT4				

6. Vulnerable versus non-vulnerable, you hold:

♠ AQT65
♥ KJ4
♦ QJ5
♣ K7

What is your opening bid?

ANSWERS

1. **Raise to 2♠** – This is an ideal three-card raise, since you have shortness in an unbid suit.

2. **Respond 1♠** – Do not bid your major suits up the line with such good spades and such poor hearts.

3. **Open 3♥** – You must take advantage of favorable vulnerability and make it difficult for the opponents to find their best spot.

4. **Respond 1♠** – Even though you have only four points, do not pass your partner's 1♣ opening with just a singleton club.

5. **Jump to 3NT** – Remember that your partner may have raised you with just three-card support. By jumping to 3NT, you give your partner a choice of games, enabling your side to play 3NT when your partner has raised you with three-card support.

6. **Open 1NT** – Describe your hand accurately in one bid.

CHAPTER 4

MORE BIDDING PRINCIPLES

A. Law of Total Trumps

According to the Law of Total Trumps*, it is safe for your side to compete to the level that corresponds to your side's total number of trumps, **almost regardless of your high card strength**. If you bid to the four-level with ten combined trumps, it is difficult for the opponents to hurt you – if the opponents double you and defeat your contract, they almost certainly could have made something their way. Your objective is to make life as difficult as possible for the opponents by bidding to the level of your total trumps immediately. Here is an example of the Law of Total Trumps in the context of a complete hand:

DLR: West   ♠ T8
VUL: None   ♥ KJ83
Swiss Teams   ♦ Q962
             ♣ K94

    ♠ AK9532   ♠ QJ6
    ♥ T7   ♥ Q9652
    ♦ 73   ♦ JT5
    ♣ J72   ♣ 63

         ♠ 74
         ♥ A4
         ♦ AK84
         ♣ AQT85

---

* For further information on the Law of Total Trumps, please read Larry Cohen's book, *To Bid or Not to Bid: The Law of Total Trumps.*

South	West	North	East
	2♠	Pass	3♠
4♣	All Pass		

East competed to the level of his side's total trumps by bidding 3♠, and look what a tough bid south has to make. Over 2♠-P-P, south would have no problem bidding 3♣, but now the 3♠ bid forces him to bid clubs at the four-level, bypassing 3NT. As it happens, N-S can make five of either minor suit on this hand, but the level of preemption forced them to guess what to do, and north guessed to pass over 4♣, which turned out to be the wrong guess. You may feel that north should bid 5♣, and you would have made the correct guess on this hand. However, the fact that you had to guess what bid to make at a high level means that the opponents' preemptive bidding has worked well for them. It is very desirable to **force the opponents to make the final guess**, and the Law of Total Trumps gives you a safety level for getting in the opponents' way and forcing them to guess what to do.

When the opponents compete against you, **do not let the opponents push you beyond the level of your total trumps**. For example, you hold:

HAND A	HAND B
♠ J65	♠ Q95
♥ Q85	♥ A865
♦ K74	♦ 5
♣ K852	♣ J8642

In each case, the auction has proceeded as follows:

Partner	RHO	You	LHO
1 ♠	Pass	2 ♠	DBL
Pass	3 ♦	?	

With Hand A, your best action is to **make a cooperative double.** In terms of points, you have close to a maximum 2♠ bid, but it is wrong to bid 3♠ **because your side has only eight trumps.** Allowing the opponents to push you to the three-level violates the Law of Total Trumps and is losing bridge tactics. Your values are just as good for defense as for offense, and the way to show a maximum 2♠ bid is to double 3♦. This is not a penalty double, since you are sitting in front of the takeout doubler. Your double says that your side has the balance of the points, and you would like your partner to do something intelligent (see Chapter Five for further information on this type of double).

On Hand B, you should compete to 3♠. Even though your side probably has only eight trumps, **you should be willing to compete to the three-level with a singleton in the opponent's suit.** It is okay to violate the Law of Total Trumps when you have a singleton or void in the opponent's long suit. This hand should play well in spades, since your partner will be able to ruff diamonds in the short trump hand.

Just as it is winning action to bid one more than the level of your total trumps with shortness in the opponent's suit, **you should bid one less than the level of your total trumps with a flat hand and no short suit.** Use the Law of Total Trumps as a guideline, but bridge judgment should always take priority.

The basic principle of the Law of Total Trumps is **don't count points, count trumps.** Here is an illustrative example:

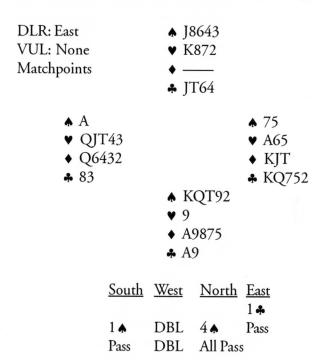

```
DLR: East            ♠ J8643
VUL: None            ♥ K872
Matchpoints          ♦ ——
                     ♣ JT64

   ♠ A                        ♠ 75
   ♥ QJT43                    ♥ A65
   ♦ Q6432                    ♦ KJT
   ♣ 83                       ♣ KQ752

                     ♠ KQT92
                     ♥ 9
                     ♦ A9875
                     ♣ A9
```

South	West	North	East
			1♣
1♠	DBL	4♠	Pass
Pass	DBL	All Pass	

West doubled the second time as a cooperative double, knowing that his side held the majority of the points. East elected to defend with his balanced minimum opening, but 4♠ could not be defeated due to the favorable club position, and E-W scored +590. This is yet another illustration that doubling on the basis of points frequently backfires because the opponents are bidding on distributional values and are able to make their doubled contract.

The Law of Total Trumps can be used as a guide to competitive bidding **before the opponents even enter the auction.** Here is a hand to illustrate this concept:

DLR: South   ♠ A84
VUL: Both   ♥ 753
Matchpoints   ♦ KJT7
                    ♣ T52

♠ KT62   ♠ QJ953
♥ Q42   ♥ A
♦ A8632   ♦ Q5
♣ J   ♣ 98764

                    ♠ 7
                    ♥ KJT986
                    ♦ 94
                    ♣ AKQ3

South	West	North	East
1♥	Pass	2♥	Pass
4♥	All Pass		

South didn't know whether or not he could make 4♥ opposite partner's raise to 2♥, but he knew that if he passed, or even if he bid 3♥, **the opponents were likely to compete in spades, against which he had limited defense.** Also, with 6-4 or 5-5 distribution, it is generally right to push for game, since this is an **offensive hand.** South therefore made a tactical jump to 4♥, which ended the auction.

The opening spade lead was won by dummy's ace, and a heart was won by east's stiff ace. A spade continuation was ruffed, and declarer continued with the king of hearts as east showed out. The ace of clubs drew west's stiff jack, and declarer now played a low club to the ten and continued clubs as west ruffed with the high queen of trumps. The spade continuation was ruffed by declarer, who had to guess diamonds in order to make the contract. East was known to have started with five spades to the QJ and the ace of hearts, **yet he never entered the auction.** With the ace of diamonds as well, east would have certainly competed in the auction. Declarer therefore played a diamond to the king to make his contract. Although E-W were never in the auction, **they were cold for 4♠**, losing one spade, one diamond and one club.

B. Picture Bidding*

Picture bidding is the process of painting your partner an accurate description of your hand based on the bidding. Suppose the auction proceeds as follows:

Opener	Responder
1♣	1♠
2♥	2NT
3♠	

A fundamental principle of bidding is that **when one hand bids three suits, he should have a singleton or void in the fourth suit.** This bidding sequence should describe **extra values and shortness in the unbid suit.** This would be a good way to describe one of two hand types: 1) a strong hand with three-card support for responder's major suit with a singleton in the fourth suit, or 2) four-card support for responder's suit and a singleton ace or king in the fourth suit. This avoids having to make a splinter bid with a stiff ace or king, which is generally undesirable. Here are typical hands for the opener to hold for this bidding sequence:

HAND A	HAND B
♠ AQ7	♠ KQT7
♥ AQJ6	♥ AQ6
♦ 5	♦ A
♣ KQ986	♣ KQ986

---

* For further information on picture bidding, I recommend Al Roth's excellent book, "Picture Bidding".

The opener's action of bidding a new suit at his second turn and then raising partner's major suit at his third turn to bid **also shows better than a minimum opening hand.** For example, suppose the opener holds any of the following three hands:

HAND C	HAND D	HAND E
♠ AQ7	♠ AQ7	♠ AQ74
♥ 5	♥ 5	♥ KT5
♦ AQJ64	♦ QJ643	♦ AQT85
♣ K874	♣ K874	♣ 2

With Hand C, after a 1♦ opening and a 1♠ response, the opener should rebid 2♣ — if partner takes a preference to 2♦ or raises to 3♣, the opener can now support spades, **showing extra values and three-card support.** If the responder passes the 2♣ rebid, the responder is showing a weak hand with long clubs, and 2♣ will be as good a spot as any to play the hand. With a minimum opening hand such as Hand D, the opener should raise partner's suit to the two-level immediately. On Hand E, if the auction proceeds 1♦-1♥-1♠-1NT, opener's 2♥ bid at his third turn shows **three-card support, shortness in the unbid suit and extra values.** Remember that the time to raise partner with three-card support is when **you can do the ruffing in the short trump hand.**

Other types of picture bids are as follows:

1. 6-5: open your 6-card suit, bid your 5-card suit twice
2. 6-4, minimum opening: rebid your 6-card suit
3. 6-4, maximum opening: open your 6-card suit, then bid your 4-card suit, and rebid your 6-card suit at your third turn, if you get a chance.

The basic principle involved in picture bidding is that **if either hand goes out of his way to bid three suits, he shows extra values and shortness in the fourth suit.**

Here are some examples showing picture bidding in action:

DLR: South
VUL: None
Rubber Bridge

<pre>
                        ♠ 6
                        ♥ JT974
                        ♦ Q8652
                        ♣ Q5
      ♠ AT54   ♠ J983
      ♥ AQ86   ♥ K532
      ♦ 74   ♦ 93
      ♣ A74   ♣ J62
                        ♠ KQ72
                        ♥ ——
                        ♦ AKJT
                        ♣ KT983
</pre>

South	West	North	East
1♣	Pass	1♥	Pass
1♠	Pass	1NT	Pass
2♦	Pass	Pass	Pass

Once south limited his hand by rebidding 1♠, he was able to bid 2♦ over 1NT to show a three-suited hand not interested in playing notrump.

DLR: South
VUL: Both
Matchpoints

<pre>
                        ♠ 84
                        ♥ AT975
                        ♦ K53
                        ♣ KT8
      ♠ K72   ♠ J53
      ♥ 863   ♥ J2
      ♦ Q94   ♦ 876
      ♣ 9743   ♣ AQ952
                        ♠ AQT96
                        ♥ KQ4
                        ♦ AJT2
                        ♣ J
</pre>

South	West	North	East
1 ♠	Pass	1NT	Pass
2 ♦	Pass	2NT	Pass
3 ♥	Pass	4 ♥	All Pass

Over north's forcing notrump response, south rebid 2♦, and when partner invited a game by rebidding 2NT, south was able to bid 3♥, showing extra values with 5-3-4-1 distribution. This enabled N-S to get to their 5-3 heart fit.

If you play forcing notrump and the opener bids 1♠, if the responder invites game by starting with a forcing 1NT and rebidding 2NT, **the opener should always bid 3♥ with a three-card heart suit** if he is accepting the game try. This enables the partnership to play in their 5-3 heart fit, since the responder will not bid a five-card heart suit.

DLR: East   ♠ A73
VUL: Both   ♥ AJ943
Matchpoints   ♦ 5
        ♣ AK62

♠ J54   ♠ KQ2
♥ K76   ♥ QT52
♦ JT983   ♦ 762
♣ 98   ♣ JT5

       ♠ T986
       ♥ 8
       ♦ AKQ4
       ♣ Q743

South	West	North	East
			Pass
Pass	Pass	1 ♥	Pass
1 ♠	Pass	2 ♣	Pass
3 ♣	Pass	3 ♠	Pass
3NT	All Pass		

North was able to show a three-suited hand with extra values and diamond shortness, and south had no problem bidding 3NT.

C. Competitive Bidding

Experience has demonstrated that certain principles should be followed in competitive auctions, which are as follows:

1) Stretch to support your partner's suit with good trump support, even if this involves a slight overbid (**Support with Support**).

2) Compete to the level of your trumps, and no further (**Law of Total Trumps**).

3) Bid your second suit in competitive auctions in order to enable your partner to make an intelligent decision whether or not to compete further.

4) Bid to the maximum level immediately and then stay out of the auction; let the opponents make the **final guess**.

We have seen examples of **Support with Support** and the **Law of Total Trumps** previously in this book. Let us take a closer look at principles (3) and (4).

In an uncontested auction, bidding a new suit after your partner has raised your major suit must be a game try or a slam try.

When the auction is competitive, however, **new suit bids do not imply an interest in slam.** The reason for the opener to bid a second suit in a competitive auction is to guide partner to the correct action if the opponents compete further. **If your side has a double fit, it is generally right to compete further; if your partner does not fit your second suit, it is probably right for your side to defend.** Here are some examples of bidding your second suit in competitive auctions:

You Hold	You	LHO	Partner	RHO
♠ K62	1♥	2♦	2♥	3♦
♥ AKQ84	?			
♦ 9				
♣ AQT5				

Bid 4♣ – You are concerned about what to do if the opponents compete over 4♥, so you are describing a game going hand with club length and strength, so that partner will be able to make an intelligent decision if the opponents take a sacrifice.

You Hold	You	LHO	Partner	RHO
♠ 6	1♥	1♠	2♥	2♠
♥ AQ962	?			
♦ Q7				
♣ AJ965				

Bid 3♣ – You are showing where your values are so that partner can make an intelligent decision if the opponents compete to 3♠. **The 3♣ bid does not create a forcing auction** – the partnership can sell out to 3♠ if neither partner has anything further to say.

You Hold	You	LHO	Partner	RHO
♠ 5	1♥	DBL	2♥	3♠
♥ AKJ753	?			
♦ KJ984				
♣ 6				

Bid 4♦ – this bid enables partner to make an informed decision when the opponents bid 4♠. Partner would compete to the five-level with a double fit in the red suits, and would defend with diamond shortness.

Here is an example of bidding your second suit in the context of a complete hand:

DLR: West
VUL: Both
Swiss Teams

♠ AQJ765
♥ K7
♦ 83
♣ AK9

♠ 4
♥ AJT986
♦ AQT4
♣ 87

♠ 98
♥ Q543
♦ K762
♣ J32

♠ KT32
♥ 2
♦ J95
♣ QT654

South	West	North	East
	1♥	DBL	2♥
2♠	3♦	4♠	5♥
Pass	Pass	5♠	All Pass

North had a strong enough hand to double and then bid spades, and when his partner freely bid 2♠, bidding a game was no problem. West made the key bid of 3♦, showing his second suit. With a double fit, east took the cheap sacrifice in 5♥, which would have been down two tricks. However, north elected to bid 5♠, which went down one on the lie of the cards.

This hand also illustrates the principle that **the five-level belongs to the opponents**. Stated simply, this means that when you have pushed the opponents to the five-level in a competitive auction, your side has a huge advantage in the bidding. Other pairs may have been allowed to play at the four-level, so if the opponents can only take ten tricks, your side will receive an excellent score, and if the opponents make eleven tricks, your side will receive an average score. Doubling when you have pushed the opponents to the five-level reduces your average score into a bottom if the opponents make their contract, and if the opponents were going down, your side was getting an excellent score anyway.

Another way to look at it is that when you have pushed the opponents to the five-level, you have two ways to gain: The opponents may be a trick too high, or they may be a trick too low.

It is to your advantage to maneuver competitive auctions so that it is the opponents and not your side who have to make the **final guess***. You know you have achieved this goal when you have bid your hand to the limit, and you don't know what the right action for the opponents is. If you don't know what the opponents' correct action is, the chances are that they have a very close decision and may very well make the wrong guess. Here are some examples of making the opponents make the final guess:

---

* The concept of making the opponents make the final guess is based on Kit Woolsey's excellent book on matchpoint play, *Matchpoints*.

You Hold	You	LHO	Partner	RHO
♠ AKJ986	1♠	2♦	2♠	3♦
♥ A8	4♠!			
♦ 76				
♣ KJ4				

Your 4♠ bid was somewhat of a stretch, but you have put the opponents in the position of having to make the final guess on the hand, namely, whether or not to sacrifice in 5♦. You don't care what they decide to do, since you have no idea whether or not 4♠ will make, and you know that if the opponents guess wrong, your side will get an excellent result. Of course, if the opponents bid 5♦, you will double the contract to prevent your partner from bidding 5♠.

You Hold	You	LHO	Partner	RHO
♠ 72	1♥	1♠	2♥	Pass
♥ AKT854	3♥			
♦ Q97				
♣ A4				

At your second turn, you can pass, bid 3♥ or bid 4♥. If you pass, there should be no question in your mind that it is right for the opponents to compete to 2♠; if you bid 4♥, the opponents' right action would be to defend, possibly doubling you. However, if you bid 3♥, **you don't really know what the correct action by the opponents** is. Consequently, the 3♥ bid forces the opponents to make the final guess, which is exactly what you want.

You Hold	LHO	Partner	RHO	You
♠ 7	1♠	2♥	DBL	5♥!
♥ J97542				
♦ 84				
♣ T743				

By jumping to 5♥ immediately, you make it difficult for the opponents to describe their hands and decide what to do. You know that it is right for them to bid over 4♥, but you don't know what the right action is over 5♥. Once again, the opponents must make the final guess.

You Hold	LHO	Partner	RHO	You
♠ AK	1♣	3♥	3♠	6♥!
♥ J97542				
♦ T743				
♣ 8				

By bidding 6♥, you put unbearable pressure on the opponents, who have to guess how high to bid. One of the opponents is virtually certain to be void in hearts, and if the opponents bid 6♠, **you can make a penalty double and collect your two trump tricks.**

D. Unusual Actions

Sometimes, the system that you are playing forces you to make an unusual bid. For example, suppose your partner opens 1NT, and you hold:

♠ QT865
♥ 6
♦ Q76
♣ KJ86

You bid 2♥ as a transfer to spades, your partner bids 2♠, what is your rebid? In Jacoby Transfers, transferring to one suit and then bidding a new suit is natural and game forcing, so you cannot rebid 3♣, which would be forcing to game. You are forced to rebid 2NT, showing a five-card spade suit and invitational values, **despite holding a singleton heart.** If your partner passes 2NT, that is where you will play it, but if your partner goes back to 3♠, showing three or more spades, you **should raise to 4♠**. Once your partner supports spades, you can upgrade the value of your hand for the singleton heart, and you now have enough to force to game opposite a strong notrump opening.

Frequently, the opponent's bidding forces you to take unusual action in order to get a good result. For example:

DLR: East   ♠ A9743
VUL: Both   ♥ 83
Matchpoints   ♦ 53
     ♣ A762

	♠ KJT86		♠ Q5
	♥ 42		♥ KJT765
	♦ QJ62		♦ K984
	♣ 93		♣ 4

     ♠ 2
     ♥ AQ9
     ♦ AT7
     ♣ KQJT85

South	West	North	East
			2♥
3NT	All Pass		

South should overcall 3NT rather than 3♣ over east's 2♥ opening bid. He has a double stopper, and a source of tricks in the club suit. A 3♣ overcall could make it difficult to get to 3NT. Do not let the spade singleton deter you from making the best available bid.

Here is another example where the opponent's bidding forces you to take unusual action:

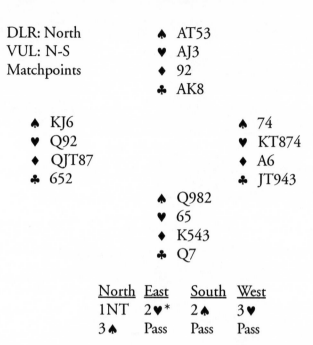

DLR: North
VUL: N-S
Matchpoints

♠ AT53
♥ AJ3
♦ 92
♣ AK8

♠ KJ6
♥ Q92
♦ QJT87
♣ 652

♠ 74
♥ KT874
♦ A6
♣ JT943

♠ Q982
♥ 65
♦ K543
♣ Q7

North	East	South	West
1NT	2♥*	2♠	3♥
3♠	Pass	Pass	Pass

East's 2♥ bid showed hearts and an unspecified minor suit. South must take action, since his side has the majority of the points, but the problem is what action to take. Unless you play negative doubles at the two-level over your partner's notrump openings, a double would be for penalties. It seems that the least-of-evils bid is to bid 2♠ on a four-card suit. This bid enabled N-S to compete successfully to 3♠ on this hand.

E. Bidding Problems

Certain hand types create bidding problems at bridge. One hand type is a 4-4-4-1 distribution with a singleton spade; another problem hand type is a hand with 4 hearts and 5 diamonds not strong enough to make a reverse bid. There is also the matter of protecting tenaces (broken honor sequences, such as KJ or AQ) in your hand from being attacked on opening lead. Here is an example of bidding to protect tenaces in your hand:

```
DLR: South              ♠ J9
VUL: Both               ♥ 9742
Matchpoints             ♦ T2
                        ♣ AQ976

      ♠ QT6                         ♠ 742
      ♥ AQT63                       ♥ J8
      ♦ AQ7                         ♦ J953
      ♣ T4                          ♣ 8532

                        ♠ AK853
                        ♥ K5
                        ♦ K864
                        ♣ KJ
```

South	West	North	East
1♠	2♥	Pass	Pass
2NT	Pass	3NT	All Pass

South had a rebid problem at his second turn – his shape wasn't right to make a reopening double, and he wanted to protect the king of hearts, so he made the slight overbid of 2NT. His partner had an easy 3NT bid, and the contract proved difficult to defeat. West led a heart to his partner's jack and declarer's king. Declarer now ran five rounds of clubs, pitching one spade and two diamonds from his hand, and west was squeezed on the fifth round of clubs. The position was as follows:

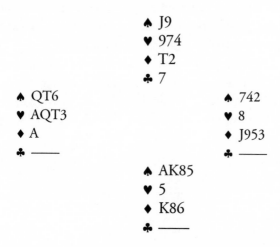

When declarer led the fifth round of clubs, east pitched the two of spades and south pitched the six of diamonds. At this point, whatever west pitches gives declarer the ninth trick. If west pitches a spade, the eight of spades becomes a winner, and if west pitches the ace of diamonds, the king becomes high. West did best by pitching a heart away, but declarer simply led a low diamond. West won the ace and cashed three rounds of hearts, but declarer claimed the last three tricks with the ace and king of spades and the king of diamonds.

Sometimes you have a rebid problem because you have a strong hand with no appropriate bid to make. Here are two examples:

DLR: South
VUL: Both
Matchpoints

```
                    ♠ AJ
                    ♥ AQ9
                    ♦ 2
                    ♣ AQJ8765
  ♠ K842                          ♠ QT97
  ♥ K75                           ♥ 64
  ♦ JT8                           ♦ AQ76
  ♣ K43                           ♣ T92
                    ♠ 653
                    ♥ JT832
                    ♦ K9543
                    ♣ ——
```

South	West	North	East
Pass	Pass	1♣	Pass
1♥	Pass	2♠!	Pass
3♦	Pass	3♥	Pass
4♥	All Pass		

South elected to respond to his partner's 1♣ opening because he didn't want to pass with a void in his partner's minor suit. North, with a difficult bid at his second turn, elected to jump shift in his two-card spade suit before jumping to 4♥, which ended the auction. On the jack of diamonds lead, declarer was able to pitch dummy's spade loser on his king of diamonds. Declarer took a successful trump finesse, played a second round of trumps, and played ace and queen of clubs, pitching two spades from his hand. West won the king of clubs, but that was the defenders' last trick. Declarer drew the last trump ending in dummy, and ran dummy's good clubs, pitching all of his diamonds.

DLR: South   ♠ AJ53
VUL: Both   ♥ AT9
Swiss Teams   ♦ KJ5
                ♣ J65

♠ 9		♠ KQT8762
♥ 76432		♥ 8
♦ 9		♦ T2
♣ AQ9843		♣ K72

                ♠ 4
                ♥ KQJ5
                ♦ AQ87643
                ♣ T

South	West	North	East
1 ♦	Pass	1 ♠	Pass
2 ♦	Pass	2 ♥	Pass
3 ♥	Pass	4 ♦	Pass
4NT	Pass	5 ♦	Pass
6 ♦	Pass	Pass	Pass

North solved his rebid problem at his second turn by bidding 2♥ as a forcing bid. When he heard his partner raise to 3♥, showing four-card heart support and a six-card or longer diamond suit, he knew that 3NT was the wrong contract and bid a forcing 4♦, easily getting to the laydown diamond slam.

F. Passed Hand Bidding

The single most important fact to remember about bidding by a passed hand is that **no bid that you make is forcing**, with the exception of cuebidding the opponent's suit, making a fit-showing jump, or making a splinter bid. Since your bid of a new suit can be passed, you must follow the principle of **Support with Sup-**

port. If your partner opens the bidding with one heart or one spade, you cannot bid a new suit if you have as many as three cards in your partner's suit, since you might be left to play in your suit when you have an eight-card major suit fit. Therefore, bidding a new suit over partner's opening bid of one heart or one spade tends to deny three-card support.

If you have support for partner's major suit, you must show it immediately. A simple raise of the major shows 6 to 9 points, and at least three-card support. If you have a limit raise in support of your partner's major suit, you should adopt the **Reverse Drury** convention. Playing Reverse Drury, a bid of 2♣ by a passed hand is artificial, and shows a limit raise with three or more trumps. The opener rebids his major suit if he is not interested in game, and any new suit bid by the opener shows game interest and is a **help-suit game try (HSGT)**. The responder should jump to game in the major with help in that suit (ace, king or shortness) and should sign off in three of the agreed major without help in that suit.

Remember that whenever your partner makes a HSGT, **you should focus on your holding in that suit.** With a good holding in that suit, you should jump to game; with a poor holding in that suit, you go back to three of partner's major suit. **Do not count points** when your partner makes a HSGT - the only important factor is your holding in that suit. Here is an example:

DLR: East   ♠ K42
VUL: N-S   ♥ 8752
Matchpoints   ♦ QJ
                   ♣ QT83

♠ J63   ♠ 8
♥ QT6   ♥ AKJ43
♦ 6532   ♦ AT94
♣ 752   ♣ K64

                   ♠ AQT975
                   ♥ 9
                   ♦ K87
                   ♣ AJ9

South	West	North	East
			1♥
1♠	Pass	2♠	DBL
3♦	Pass	4♠	All Pass

East made a reopening double over 2♠, showing spade short-ness and three-card or longer support for all other suits. South bid 3♦ as a HSGT – with three potential diamond losers, this is the suit that he needed help in. Note that HSGT's also apply after you have overcalled, and may apply in a competitive auction – the opener may be bidding a second suit, or is making a HSGT, and clarifies his intentions on his next bid. In this case, south's 3♦ was a HSGT, and north had an easy jump to 4♠, which makes eleven tricks with a successful club finesse.

Playing Reverse Drury, responder's jump to three of the major after having passed initially is **preemptive**, with four or more trumps. You are trying to shut the opponents out of the bidding. A hand such as:

♠ 984
♥ KT95
♦ 64
♣ QT76

would qualify for a jump to 3♥ over partner's one heart opening after you had passed initially. Since you would bid 2♣ with a good hand, you can jump to three of partner's major with a weak hand and four-card trump support. Remember that the **Law of Total Trumps** protects you when you make these types of bids.

There is only one reason for a passed hand to jump in a new suit, which is that your hand has improved dramatically as a result of partner's opening bid. A jump in a new suit should be a **Fit-Showing Jump**, showing at least five cards in the suit that you are jumping in and at least four-card support for partner's suit. Instead of making a Drury 2♣ bid as a general game try, you can tell your partner that you have at least nine cards in two suits, and partner can better evaluate his hand in terms of going to game or even to slam. Here is an example of hands that should make a **Fit-Showing Jump** after you have passed and partner has opened 1♥ in third seat:

HAND A	HAND B
♠ 643	♠ 643
♥ Q976	♥ KT76
♦ AQJ85	♦ 5
♣ 4	♣ AK865

Hand A reevaluates into a limit raise in support of hearts, and you should jump to 3♦ to show a four-card limit raise and a five-card diamond suit. Partner will realize that the king of diamonds is a golden card, and that honor cards in spades and clubs are not worth that much. With a minimum opening, partner will rebid 3♥ and you will pass. Hand B reevaluates into 14 points in support of hearts. You should bid 3♣ as a **Fit-Showing Jump**, but even if partner signs off in 3♥, you should bid a game anyway. You should have a reasonable play for game opposite any hand close to an opening bid.

There is no reason to play a jump by a passed hand in a new suit as preemptive, **since that hand has already had a chance to preempt** and failed to do so. Fit-Showing Jumps apply even if the opponents compete. In fact, it is more important than ever to show your fit when the auction is about to become competitive.

G. <u>Balancing</u>

You are in the **balancing seat** if your pass would end the auction. You should often compete with less-than-normal high card strength in the balancing seat rather than let the opponents play the hand at a low level. All of your bids in balancing seat can be made with approximately three points less than the corresponding bid in direct seat.

The first situation we will look at is as follows: LHO opens one of a suit and there are two passes to you. It will rarely be best for your side to let the opponents have the contract, unless you have length and strength in their suit. If your hand is suitable for either a takeout double or an overcall, there will be no problem. However, you will frequently be dealt a hand that would not have acted in the direct position. Since partner may have an excellent hand – it is relatively common for your partner to have opening bid strength, with a hand that was unable to overcall or double in direct seat – you want to keep the bidding open whenever possible.

A takeout double can be made with less than opening values in the balancing seat. Experts would disagree on just how weak one can be, but most bridge players would expect a minimum of nine or ten points with support for all unbid suits. While the balancing double can be quite light, it is unlimited in strength, and should be used with any hand too strong for direct action. Here are two examples of hands that should take action after the bidding has proceeded 1♣-P-P to you:

HAND A   HAND B
♠ K654   ♠ AQJ98
♥ J762   ♥ K6
♦ AJ87   ♦ AKJ5
♣ 5   ♣ 97

You should make a takeout double with each of these hands. With Hand A, you are happy with whatever suit partner bids. Bear in mind that partner may have a very good hand that could not act in direct position because the opponents opened his best suit. With Hand B, you are doubling before mentioning your spades to indicate extra strength.

Bidding a new suit in the balancing seat normally shows a five-card or longer suit, but you may occasionally balance with a four-card suit at the one-level if other alternatives seem even less attractive. A simple non-jump bid at the one- or two-level no longer promises opening bid values, but should show 8-13 points. A jump bid in a new suit in the balancing seat is not preemptive, but instead should show a good six-card or longer suit and 14-17 points. Here are some examples of balancing bids after the bidding has gone 1♥-P-P to you:

HAND A   HAND B   HAND C
♠ AQJ4   ♠ 65   ♠ KQJ876
♥ 654   ♥ 87   ♥ A5
♦ 43   ♦ AJT976   ♦ KJ6
♣ K543   ♣ K65   ♣ 98

Although both Hands A and B would have passed in direct seat, you should balance with both of these hands. On Hand A, you should bid 1♠, even though it is only a four-card suit. It is better than making a takeout double without diamond support, or selling out to 1♥. On Hand B, you should bid 2♦. Partner may hope you have more points and bid too much, but there is no reasonable option. With hand C, you should **jump to 2♠**. This is an example of what a jump overcall in the balancing position looks like. As the opponents have already passed the hand out at the one-level, this meaning is much more useful than defining the jump as preemptive.

A 1NT bid in the balancing seat is defined very differently from the direct position. Rather than the normal 15-17 points required in direct seat, the balancing 1NT shows only about 11-14 points over LHO's opening bid of one of a minor, and 11-16 points over LHO's opening bid of one of a major. The reason why this range is higher when LHO opens with a major suit is because if you double first, partner will probably bid a new suit at the two-level, either 2♣ or 2♦. Now you must bid 2NT, and doubling first and then bidding 2NT on a balanced 15-16 point hand can get you too high if your partner has a weak hand. On the other hand, when your LHO opens with a minor suit, you can double first and then bid 1NT over partner's expected response of 1♥ or 1♠.

If you have a balanced hand without a five-card suit or without support for all of the unbid suits, you will have no call available to you except for a balancing notrump bid. For example, the auction is 1♦-P-P to you, and you hold:

♠ K3
♥ J54
♦ KJ65
♣ A975

In the direct position, you would have passed. In the balancing seat, you certainly do not want to sell out to 1♦, and you cannot make a takeout double, so you must be able to bid 1NT with this type of hand.

What do you do if you have a real notrump overcall? In the balancing seat, you must double first, and then bid notrump at the cheapest available level to describe this type of hand. This shows 15-17 points over a minor suit opening and 17-18 points over a major suit opening. An immediate jump to 2NT in the balancing position should show about 19-21 points and a balanced hand. Note that this is **not** an "Unusual Notrump" bid in this position.

Balancing When The Opponents Have Found A Fit

If the opponents have found a fit, and are about to stop comfortably at the two-level, it usually pays to balance. In particular, if the auction begins with 1 of a suit – Pass – 2 of same suit – Pass – Pass back to you, you should be reluctant to sell out cheaply. Do not think that because you didn't have enough to act at the one-level, you can't possibly have enough to bid now. When you hear this auction, your first thought should be, "I want to balance. The opponents have found a fit, so our side must also have a fit." Now you will look at your hand and see what bid you can come up with.

If you are not vulnerable, you may choose to act even though you don't have many points. **It is always up to the hand with shortness in the opponent's suit to act in this type of balancing auction**. If you are short in the opponent's suit, you may make a takeout double with very few points if you have tolerance for all of the unbid suits. It can even be acceptable to balance with a four-card suit at the two-level if a takeout double is out of the question. A balancing bid of 2NT in this situation is still "unusual", but may be done with 5-4 in the minors, as opposed to the normally required 5-5.

Be wary of balancing when the opponents have not found a fit. You must always diagnose the opponents' auction. Just because the opponents stop at a low level does not always make it safe to balance. The key question you must ask yourself is, "Do the opponents have an eight-card or longer fit?" If so, that means that **your side must have a fit also**, and this makes it safe to balance. If the opponents' auction indicates that they have a misfit, beware of balancing. If the hand is a misfit for the opponents, it is a misfit for your side as well, and good opponents will not hesitate to double you with a majority of the high card points and no fit. Here are two examples of auctions where the opponents do not have a fit, where it would be dangerous to balance:

LHO	RHO		LHO	RHO
1♠	1NT		1♥	1♠
2♦	2♠		2♣	2♥

In each of these hands, the responder has taken a preference to the opener's first bid suit. The opponents do not necessarily have a fit, so the chances are that your side does not have a fit either, and it would be very dangerous to balance on this type of auction.

There are two good things that can happen to you by balancing. The less likely outcome is that you will reach a makeable contract. The more common outcome is that you will push the opponents one level higher and they will go down one. **This should be seen as your major goal**. Therefore, when your partner balances and pushes the opponents one level higher, **do not "punish partner"** by bidding further, unless you have extraordinary support for your partner's suit. Remember that your partner has already bid your cards for you when he balanced. In most cases when your partner balances, you should discount your first ten points, as your partner has already assumed that you hold that much.

Here is an example of balancing in the context of a complete hand:

DLR: West   ♠ J86
VUL: Both   ♥ 654
Matchpoints   ♦ A8
       ♣ A8762

  ♠ QT9   ♠ K754
  ♥ KQ2   ♥ 873
  ♦ KQ63   ♦ T752
  ♣ T94   ♣ Q3

      ♠ A32
      ♥ AJT9
      ♦ J94
      ♣ KJ5

South	West	North	East
	1♦	Pass	Pass
1NT	All Pass		

South's best bid over 1♦-P-P is to bid a balancing 1NT **despite not having a diamond stopper.** With 4-3-3-3 distribution, the hand is not suitable to a takeout double, and bidding 1NT has the virtue of describing a balanced hand in the 11- to 14-point range. Declarer ducked the opening 3 of diamonds lead to his jack and, with dummy's club suit coming home, took 9 tricks (5 clubs, 2 diamonds, 1 heart and 1 spade) for a top score.

Here is another example of a successful balancing auction:

DLR: South
VUL: N-S
Matchpoints

♠ KT865
♥ 942
♦ K43
♣ 75

♠ Q7
♥ AQT83
♦ Q2
♣ 9843

♠ AJ92
♥ K76
♦ 985
♣ KJ2

♠ 43
♥ J5
♦ AJT76
♣ AQT6

South	West	North	East
1 ♦	Pass	1 ♠	Pass
2 ♣	Pass	2 ♦	Pass
Pass	2 ♥	All Pass	

When north took a preference to 2♦, west elected to balance on his five-card heart suit. 2♥ made exactly eight tricks, and south must guess the position of the queen of diamonds in order to make 3♦.

If N-S compete further to 3♦, **east should not bid 3♥**. When west balanced with 2♥, he already bid his partner's cards. The balancing action has succeeded when the opponents have been pushed up one level higher than they wanted to be. Therefore, the partner of the balancing bidder must be very careful not to bid further.

KEY POINTS

1. Compete to the level of your side's total trumps immediately, and then stop bidding. Let the opponents make the "final guess".

2. In a competitive auction, do not let the opponents push you beyond the level of your side's total trumps. If your side has the majority of the points, make a cooperative double and let your partner decide what to do.

3. When one hand bids three suits, this shows shortness in the fourth suit (zero or one card) and extra values.

4. In competitive auctions, bidding a second suit does not imply extra values. You are giving your partner information so that he can make an intelligent decision should the opponents compete further.

5. The five-level belongs to the opponents. Once you push the opponents to the five-level, you should generally not compete any further.

6. Particularly at matchpoints, you must sometimes make unusual bids in order to get a good result.

7. You should be very careful to play the contract from the right side, in order to protect tenaces in either your hand or your partner's hand.

8. When you are a passed hand, you must follow the principle of Support with Support. If you bid a minor suit at the two-level as a passed hand over partner's opening bid of 1♥ or 1♠, this denies three-card support for partner's suit, since your bid is not forcing. Two useful conventions to adopt by a passed hand are Reverse Drury and Fit-Showing Jumps.

9. When you are in balancing seat, you can bid with approximately three points less than what you would need to have in direct seat. If the opponents have found a fit and subsided at a low level, you should want to make a balancing bid to push them up one level higher. However, if the hand is a misfit, you should be very wary of balancing.

10. If your partner makes a balancing bid, he has already bid your cards. Do not "punish" partner for balancing by bidding again, unless you have exceptional distribution and good trump support.

BIDDING QUIZ

1. Both vulnerable, you hold:

	Partner	RHO	You	LHO
♠ 632	1♥	Pass	2♥	DBL
♥ Q85	Pass	3♦	?	
♦ K94				
♣ AT65				

2. None vulnerable, you hold:

	You	LHO	Partner	RHO
♠ 4	1♥	1♠	2♥	2♠
♥ AQ986	?			
♦ 84				
♣ AQJ74				

3. Vulnerable versus non-vulnerable, you hold:

	Partner	RHO	You	LHO
♠ 983	1♣	Pass	?	
♥ Q76				
♦ AQ83				
♣ J95				

4. Non-vulnerable versus vulnerable, you hold:

	You	LHO	Partner	RHO
♠ K96	Pass	Pass	1♠	Pass
♥ Q4	?			
♦ AQ964				
♣ 863				

5. None vulnerable, you hold:

	LHO	Partner	RHO	You
♠ K8	1♦	Pass	Pass	?
♥ QT76				
♦ AQ8				
♣ QJ42				

6. Both vulnerable, you hold:

	LHO	Partner	RHO	You
♠ A764	1♥	Pass	2♥	Pass
♥ Q86	Pass	3♦	3♥	?
♦ KQT				
♣ Q74				

ANSWERS

1. **Double** – Your double is cooperative and tells partner that your side has the majority of the points. Your partner will decide whether to bid 3♥ or leave the double in for penalties. Do not allow yourself to get pushed to the three-level with only eight trumps.

2. **Bid 3♣** – In a competitive auction, bidding a second suit enables partner to make an intelligent decision should the opponents compete further, and does not show extra values.

3. **Bid 1♦** – With nothing in spades and Qxx of hearts, you would prefer that your partner be the declarer in notrump. Therefore, respond 1♦ and hope that your partner can rebid notrump, in order to protect your partner's major suit tenaces.

4. **Bid 2♣**, Reverse Drury – You have a limit raise in support of spades, and the way you show a limit raise by a passed hand is to make a Drury bid. Under no circumstances should you bid 2♦, as this would deny three-card spade support.

5. **Bid 1NT** – In balancing seat, a 1NT bid over the opponent's minor suit opening shows 11 to 14 points and a balanced hand.

6. **Pass** – Your partner has already bid your hand when he competed to 3♦. Bidding again would be punishing partner for his enterprise in pushing the opponents up one level higher.

CHAPTER 5

TYPES OF DOUBLES

A. <u>Negative Doubles</u>

Negative doubles apply when your partner opens at the one-level with a suit bid and your RHO overcalls in another suit. A **double** by the responder shows values but denies the ability to freely bid a new suit. For example, suppose the auction proceeds as follows:

<u>Partner</u>	<u>RHO</u>	<u>You</u>
1 ♦	1 ♠	?

In order to bid a new suit at the two-level (2♣ or 2♥), you need to have both a five-card or longer suit and eleven or more points. If you are lacking either or both of these requirements, you must make a negative double.

The negative doubler generally has at least four cards in any unbid major suit. It is not necessary to have four cards in an unbid minor suit, as long as you have a convenient rebid should opener respond in that suit. For example, over 1♣-1♠, you should make a negative double with each of the following hands:

HAND A	HAND B	HAND C
♠ 863	♠ 83	♠ 83
♥ AQ84	♥ AQT76	♥ AT76
♦ KQ7	♦ 953	♦ 852
♣ K943	♣ Q53	♣ QJ64

Notice that none of these three hands contains four cards in diamonds, the unbid minor suit. If partner bids 2♦ over your negative double, you should cuebid 2♠ with Hand A, asking partner to bid notrump with a spade stopper. With an opening hand facing an opening hand, you cannot make any bid that is not forcing, and cuebidding the opponent's suit will get you to 3NT whenever your partner has a spade stopper. On Hand B, you should bid 2♥, showing five or more hearts and less than eleven points. Notice that making a negative double and then bidding a suit is a weaker action than bidding the suit directly at the two-level. On Hand C, you should bid 3♣, taking a preference to partner's first bid suit.

The higher the level of your RHO's overcall, the more points you need to make a negative double. **There is no upper point limit to a negative double.** Minimum point requirements for a negative double are as follows:

- RHO overcalls at the one level: 7 points
- RHO overcalls at the two level: 9 points
- RHO overcalls at the three level: 11 points

Please note that negative doubles apply only when partner opens the bidding with a suit at the one-level, and RHO overcalls in a suit. If RHO overcalls 1NT, all doubles are for penalty, and bidding a new suit shows a weak hand with a long suit. If partner opens with a bid that limits his hand, such as 1NT or a preemptive bid, and your RHO bids a new suit, **all doubles are for penalty.**

Here are some examples of negative doubles in the context of an entire hand:

DLR: South
VUL: Both
Matchpoints

♠ AT62
♥ T9
♦ 7
♣ KT9765

♠ J3
♥ AJ863
♦ JT84
♣ Q4

♠ KQ9
♥ KQ754
♦ 63
♣ J82

♠ 8754
♥ 2
♦ AKQ952
♣ A3

South	West	North	East
1♦	1♥	DBL	4♥
4♠	All Pass		

North's negative double enabled his side to get to their cold 20-point game. The way to keep control of the trump suit when you have the ace and are missing all of the remaining spot cards is to **duck a round of trumps early**. On this hand, declarer ruffed the second heart lead and ducked a spade in both hands. On a minor suit continuation, declarer won and played the ace of trumps, reducing the opponents to one high trump still outstanding. Declarer now went about his business of establishing the diamond suit, conceding the opponent's high trump trick whenever they wanted it.

Notice that if declarer plays the ace of spades and another spade, east can draw a third round of trumps, taking out declarer's last trump. A heart continuation forces dummy to ruff with the last outstanding trump. When the diamonds do not divide 3-3, declarer cannot make the hand.

DLR: South
VUL: Both
Matchpoints

♠ A9
♥ AQ65
♦ QJ7
♣ JT63

♠ KQT73
♥ 83
♦ KT4
♣ 974

♠ J864
♥ 974
♦ A652
♣ 82

♠ 52
♥ KJT2
♦ 983
♣ AKQ5

South	West	North	East
1♣	1♠	DBL	3♠
Pass	Pass	DBL	Pass
4♥	Pass	Pass	Pass

Over north's negative double, east jumped to 3♠ preemptively with four-card trump support. South would have bid 3♥ over a 2♠ bid from east, but over the preemptive jump to 3♠, south was forced to pass with a minimum opening bid. North now doubled again, **showing a negative double with extra values.**South was now able to bid 4♥, knowing that his partner had a good hand. Declarer made the contract by leading up to dummy's diamond honors twice, eventually making one diamond trick.

Whenever you double and then double again at your second turn, you show extra values for your initial double. If your first double was negative, your second double **is still a negative double** with extra values; if your first double was takeout, your second double **is still a takeout double** with extra values. The nature of your double never changes!

Negative doubles generally show 4-4 or 5-4 distribution in the two unbid suits. Do not make a negative double with 6-5 or

similar distribution in the unbid suits, as this gives your partner
the wrong impression of your hand. With a distributional two-
suited hand, you are better off bidding your two suits. Here is an
example:

DLR: North   ♠ A53
VUL: Both   ♥ AJ852
Swiss Teams   ◆ Q6
        ♣ J43

♠ T62   ♠ KJ
♥ KQ97   ♥ 643
◆ KT42   ◆ AJ9875
♣ T8   ♣ K2

       ♠ Q9874
       ♥ T
       ◆ 3
       ♣ AQ9765

North	East	South	West
1♥	2◆	3♣	3◆
Pass	Pass	3♠	Pass
4♠	Pass	Pass	Pass

With 6-5 distribution, south properly bid out his shape rather
than make a negative double. Remember that 6-5 distributions
are very powerful offensive hands, and you don't need much from
your partner to make a game — 6-5, **Come Alive!**

When you have a penalty double of your RHO's suit, you
must pass and wait for your partner to make a reopening double.
Whenever your partner is short in the opponent's suit, your partner is expected to make a reopening double, which shows shortness in the opponent's suit and three-card or longer support for
each of the other suits. You convert this double into a penalty
double by passing. Here are some examples of reopening doubles:

HAND A	HAND B	HAND C	HAND D
♠ AQJ75	♠ AQJ75	♠ AQ875	♠ AQJ75
♥ AQ73	♥ K764	♥ AJ73	♥ K6
♦ 4	♦ 4	♦ ———	♦ A754
♣ Q87	♣ A87	♣ KJ74	♣ 54

In each case, you have opened the bidding 1♠, your RHO has overcalled 2♦, and there are two passes back to you. With Hands A, B and C, you should make a reopening double – you have shortness in the opponent's suit, at least three-card support for each of the other suits, and you would like partner to bid his longest suit. If partner has a trump stack behind the 2♦ overcaller, he will convert your double into a penalty double by passing.

On Hand D, you should pass the 2♦ bid. You have too many diamonds to make a reopening double, and partner is marked with a weak hand. With length in the opponent's overcalled suit, you should just pass and defend.

Here is an example of a reopening double in the context of a complete hand:

DLR: North
VUL: Both
Matchpoints

	♠ T986
	♥ QT6
	♦ 543
	♣ J63

♠ K73		♠ AQ4
♥ 52		♥ AJ943
♦ KJ96		♦ 2
♣ QT85		♣ K972

	♠ J52
	♥ K87
	♦ AQT87
	♣ A4

North	East	South	West
Pass	1♥	2♦	Pass
Pass	DBL	All Pass	

With length and strength in the opponent's suit, west passes at his first turn. East reopens with a double, and west converts the double into a penalty double by passing.

Most of the time, a negative double promises four cards in any unbid major. However, you must be able to show values, and sometimes you may have only three cards in the unbid major. Remember that the purpose of making a negative double is to show a hand with values and no convenient bid to make, and you must be flexible. Here is an example of a **flexible negative double**:

You hold: ♠ 64 ♥ Q85 ♦ K9653 ♣ KJ6

Your partner opens 1♣, your RHO overcalls 1♠, and it is your call. If you cannot make a negative double because that would promise four hearts, then you are forced to pass with this hand. You do not have enough points or a strong enough suit to freely bid 2♦. Now if your LHO raises his partner to 2♠, you are shut out of the auction, despite the fact that your side has most of the high card points. It would be a wild stab in the dark to now bid 3♦ over the 2♠ bid. It is much better to make a negative double initially over your RHO's 1♠ overcall in order to show values. If your partner bids 2♥ over the negative double, you are willing to play in a 4-3 fit. Remember that the time it is desirable to play in a 4-3 fit is **when the short trump hand can ruff losers**. Since your partner will be ruffing his spade losers in the short trump hand, playing in a 4-3 fit will play very well on this hand.

Here is an example of a flexible negative double in the context of an entire hand:

DLR: South   ♠ AJ2
VUL: Both   ♥ 653
Matchpoints   ♦ Q42
              ♣ AJT9

```
          ♠ AJ2
          ♥ 653
          ♦ Q42
          ♣ AJT9
♠ T7                      ♠ K9654
♥ AKJ92                   ♥ QT87
♦ J9                      ♦ T83
♣ 7654                    ♣ 3
          ♠ Q83
          ♥ 4
          ♦ AK765
          ♣ KQ82
```

South	West	North	East
1♦	1♥	DBL	3♥
4♣	Pass	5♣	All Pass

Without a flexible negative double to show values, north cannot make an intelligent bid over RHO's 1♥ overcall.

B. Responsive Doubles

A basic principle of competitive bidding is that whenever the opponents bid and raise the same suit, **all doubles are for takeout**. The reason for this is that once the opponents have found a fit, our side also probably has a fit somewhere, and using double as takeout to show the unbid suits will occur much more frequently than a penalty double.

A **responsive double** is a competitive takeout double used by the partner of the overcaller or the doubler, after the opponents have bid and raised the same suit. The responsive double is used to show values in the unbid suits without a biddable suit of one's own, and tends to deny primary support for partner's suit.

There are two types of responsive doubles. The first type is when LHO has opened the bidding with a suit bid, partner makes a takeout double, and RHO raises his partner's suit. For example:

LHO	Partner	RHO	You
1♥	DBL	2♥	?

HAND A	HAND B	HAND C
♠ J54	♠ 75	♠ 75
♥ 83	♥ 964	♥ 64
♦ AJ96	♦ AQ74	♦ AJ84
♣ K862	♣ KT64	♣ Q9853

LHO	Partner	RHO	You
1♦	DBL	3♦	?

HAND D	HAND E	HAND F
♠ Q975	♠ A64	♠ A964
♥ KJ62	♥ AJ6	♥ J863
♦ 83	♦ 832	♦ K2
♣ A76	♣ Q954	♣ Q54

You should make a responsive double with all six of these hands. The responsive double is used to show a hand with values to take some action but no clearcut bid to make. Note that when the opponents have bid and raised a major suit, making a responsive double **tends to deny four cards in the other major**. Holding four cards in the other major, you should bid your major suit rather than make a responsive double.

The second type of responsive double occurs when LHO opens the bidding with a suit bid, partner overcalls in a suit, and RHO raises his partner's suit. For example:

LHO	Partner	RHO	You
1♣	1♠	3♣	?

HAND A	HAND B	HAND C
♠ Q4	♠ 83	♠ 83
♥ KJ985	♥ QJT32	♥ AK32
♦ A8743	♦ AK74	♦ Q76532
♣ 6	♣ 63	♣ 6

Each of these three hands should make a responsive double to show values and the two unbid suits.

Just as with negative doubles, responsive doubles should not be made with highly distributional hands (6-5 or better in two suits). These hands should be bid naturally. Also, just as for negative doubles, there is no maximum point count limitation to make a responsive double. Since the takeout doubler has asked his partner to bid a suit, the responsive doubler simply throws the decision of what suit to bid back to his partner, who made the initial takeout double.

The partner of the responsive doubler does have the option of passing the responsive double, thereby converting it into a penalty double. You should do this with no long suit of your own to bid and length and strength in the opponent's suit. Sometimes the partner of the responsive doubler passes with a lot of high card points and no long suit, collecting a sure profit when no fit exists.

When you have overcalled in a suit and your partner has made a responsive double, the overcaller rebids as follows:

- Bid one of the unbid suits with four or more cards.
- Rebid a six-card or good five-card suit with no fit in the unbid suits.
- Bid notrump with one or more stoppers in the opponent's suit.
- Pass with honors in the opponent's suit and no fit in partner's suit, converting the responsive double into a penalty double.
- Bid a reasonable three-card suit with a minimum overcall and a weak suit.

Here are some examples of responsive doubles in the context of a complete hand:

DLR: East
VUL: None
Matchpoints

                    ♠ A43
                    ♥ J7
                    ♦ KQ6
                    ♣ Q9853

♠ QT765   ♠ 2
♥ 985   ♥ AQT632
♦ 5   ♦ T832
♣ K642   ♣ J7

                    ♠ KJ98
                    ♥ K4
                    ♦ AJ974
                    ♣ AT

South	West	North	East
			2♥
DBL	3♥	DBL	Pass
3NT	All Pass		

North is able to make a responsive double over west's 3♥ bid, enabling N-S to get to 3NT, which is the only makeable game. Notice that 5♣ or 5♦ has no chance.

DLR: East
VUL: N-S
Swiss Teams

```
                    ♠ 83
                    ♥ AKJ7
                    ♦ 98
                    ♣ QJT93

    ♠ AT76                          ♠ KQJ954
    ♥ T863                          ♥ Q92
    ♦ AT52                          ♦ 63
    ♣ 8                             ♣ 74

                    ♠ 2
                    ♥ 54
                    ♦ KQJ74
                    ♣ AK652
```

South	West	North	East
			2♠
3♦	4♠	DBL	Pass
5♣	All Pass		

Without a responsive double, north has no good bid available. Bidding 5♣ would be a wild shot in the dark, and would miss a possible 4-4 heart fit. Doubling 4♠ for penalties would result in down two for +300, which is inadequate compensation for a vulnerable game. North's responsive double made it easy for his side to get to the right game.

Here is a spectacular example of a responsive double by the opening bidder:

DLR: North   ♠ QT
VUL: None   ♥ KQ4
Matchpoints   ♦ T
                    ♣ AKQJ842

♠ K8762   ♠ 93
♥ AJ52   ♥ 9873
♦ 864   ♦ AK9732
♣ 5   ♣ 7

                    ♠ AJ54
                    ♥ T6
                    ♦ QJ5
                    ♣ T963

North	East	South	West
1♣	2♦	DBL	3♦
DBL	Pass	3NT	All Pass

North's double was responsive, showing **extra values with no four-card major suit**. This bid enabled N-S to get to 3NT, the only making game.

These examples illustrate the importance of responsive doubles in competitive auctions. Generally, responsive doubles are played to the same level as negative doubles, even though they are independent of one another.

C. Cooperative Doubles

The positional factor is very important in determining whether a double is for penalties or for takeout. If you are defending and your holding in the trump suit is AQT5, you might take three trump tricks if you are sitting behind the declarer; with this same holding, you could be limited to only one trump trick if you are sitting in front of the declarer. For this reason, **doubling behind, or over the bidder is generally for penalties,** whereas **doubling in front of, or under the bidder is more takeout oriented.**

There is a type of double that is neither a penalty double nor a takeout double. This type of double is called a **cooperative double**, and is made in front of the bidder. The message that is conveyed by a cooperative double is, "Partner, we have the balance of the points, but I am not sure of what action to take. Please do something intelligent."

The double in front of the overcaller does not show a trump stack, as does the double behind the overcaller. The double simply shows a fair balanced hand, no great fit for partner's suit, and the balance of the points. Usually, the doubler has length (two or more cards) but no great strength in the overcaller's suit.

Let us look at a few examples of cooperative doubles:

1. ♠ 98	Partner	RHO	You	LHO
♥ J52	1♠	Pass	2♣	2♥
♦ AJ6	Pass	Pass	DBL	
♣ AQ875				

Many players would be stuck for a bid at this point in the auction. A cooperative double provides the perfect solution — you have length but no strength in the opponent's suit, and your side has the balance of the points.

2. ♠ QT87	Partner	RHO	You	LHO
♥ K63	1♥	Pass	2♥	3♣
♦ KJ84	Pass	Pass	DBL	
♣ 72				

You have a maximum 2♥ bid, but bidding 3♥ in this auction would be very wrong. A 3♥ bid would violate the Law of Total Trumps - your side has only eight combined trumps, so why go the three-level? Rather than letting the opponents push you to the three-level, you should make a cooperative double and tell your partner that your side has the balance of the points. If your partner has a trump trick, he will be delighted to pass, and if not, partner can always bid 3♥.

3. ♠ QJ85   Partner   RHO   You   LHO
    ♥ 74   1♦   Pass   1♠   2♥
    ♦ T82   Pass   Pass   DBL
    ♣ AQ97

Since your cooperative double promises at least two cards in the opponent's suit, your partner can leave the double in with a minimum opening and one or more trump tricks. You would bid the same way with a five-card spade suit, since your partner would tend to bid 2♠ with three-card support rather than pass the double.

Here is an example of a cooperative double in the context of an entire hand:

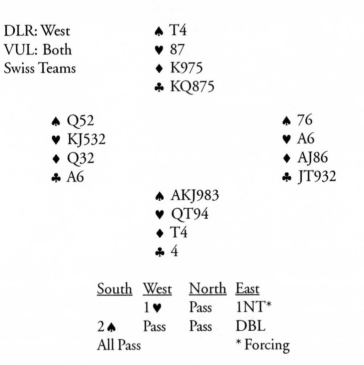

DLR: West   ♠ T4
VUL: Both   ♥ 87
Swiss Teams   ♦ K975
                   ♣ KQ875

♠ Q52   ♠ 76
♥ KJ532   ♥ A6
♦ Q32   ♦ AJ86
♣ A6   ♣ JT932

                   ♠ AKJ983
                   ♥ QT94
                   ♦ T4
                   ♣ 4

        South   West   North   East
                1♥   Pass   1NT*
        2♠   Pass   Pass   DBL
        All Pass   * Forcing

After starting with a forcing notrump response, east reopened with a cooperative double over south's 2♠ bid, showing values and no clear action to take. With a likely trump trick, west converted his partner's double to penalties by passing. West led a diamond to his partner's jack, and east shifted to a trump at trick two. This resulted in down two doubled – E-W went +500 on a partscore hand.

Here is an example of a situation that occurs frequently at matchpoints:

```
DLR: East        ♠ K42
VUL: None        ♥ T85
Matchpoints      ♦ K842
                 ♣ AJ3

♠ AT5                          ♠ J9
♥ Q92                          ♥ AJ764
♦ QJ                           ♦ AT3
♣ T8752                        ♣ K94

                 ♠ Q8763
                 ♥ K3
                 ♦ 9765
                 ♣ Q6
```

South	West	North	East
			1♥
Pass	2♥	Pass	Pass
2♠	DBL	All Pass	

When the opponents stopped in 2♥, south made a balancing bid of 2♠. Obviously, not everyone would make this balancing bid, and west doubled to show a maximum 2♥ bid. East elected to pass, not wishing to bid 3♥ with his minimum opening and poor heart spots. The result was down two for +300 and a top score for E-W, who can only make nine tricks in hearts.

If you make these cooperative doubles when the opponents balance against you, you will find that your opponents become more reluctant to balance against you for fear of getting doubled, and they fail to balance against you when they should.

There is another type of cooperative double that occurs when you jump to game with a good hand, and the opponents compete over your bid. A double in this situation is saying, "Partner, I bid game expecting to make it. Either support my suit to the next level, or leave the double in if you have some defense and you don't fit my suit." This type of double most emphatically **does not imply anything in the opponent's trump suit.** It shows that you had a good hand for your game bid, and not just a long suit with a weak hand. Some examples of this type of cooperative double are as follows:

1. ♠ AJ5   RHO   You   LHO   Partner
   ♥ AKQJ753   1♦   4♥   5♦   Pass
   ♦ 3   Pass   DBL
   ♣ K7

With an ace or some values in the black suits, or unexpected heart length, partner should bid 5♥. With a yarborough or a weak hand, partner should pass and hope to take three or more tricks on defense.

2. ♠ 4   Partner RHO   You   LHO
   ♥ AQJT763   Pass   Pass   4♥   4♠
   ♦ A4   Pass   Pass   DBL
   ♣ K76

This example is taken from Kit Woolsey's excellent book, "Matchpoints". Your 4♥ bid is not a classic preempt, but it is a reasonable tactic opposite a passed hand and puts the opponents under a lot of pressure. When your LHO bids 4♠, you can't just sit there and pass with your strong hand, and you have no reason to believe that you can make 5♥ and bid again at the five-level. The answer is to make a cooperative double, showing a good hand for your 4♥ opening, and let your partner decide what to do.

3. ♠ 64	LHO	Partner	RHO	You
♥ AQ854	2♠	DBL	Pass	4♥
♦ AJ6	Pass	Pass	4♠	DBL
♣ 632				

Your double of 4♠ shows that your jump to 4♥ was based on high cards rather than a weak hand with a long heart suit. Your double does not command partner to pass; on the contrary, it encourages your partner to compete further at the five-level if he holds the right hand.

D. Takeout Doubles

In order to make a takeout double, there are four requirements:

1) Shortness in the opponent's suit (two or fewer cards)
2) At least three-card support for each of the unbid suits
3) Thirteen or more points, including distribution points
4) No five-card major

Let us analyze these requirements. The first requirement is that you must be short in the opponent's suit. If you have three or more cards in the suit that your RHO has opened, **your hand is unsuitable for a takeout double.** With length in the opponent's suit, you must either pass or overcall in notrump. On some occasions, your only reasonable action is to overcall in a good four-card suit. For example, your RHO opens 1♦, and you hold:

♠ AKJ6
♥ Q72
♦ K76
♣ 643

It is perfectly acceptable to overcall 1♠ with your nice four-card suit. Overcalling 1♠ satisfies all three purposes of an overcall (see page 25).

The second requirement caters to the fact that your partner will bid his longest suit in response to your takeout double. If you make a takeout double without support for one of the unbid suits, your short suit is the suit that your partner is likeliest to respond in. You will then be placed in an untenable position: You will either have to pass with inadequate trump support, or you will bid your own suit over partner's response, **which promises extra values**. If you don't have the extra values that you promise, you will get too high, and a disaster will ensue. For example, suppose your RHO opens 1♦, and you hold:

♠ AQ853
♥ K962
♦ 52
♣ A7

Do not make a takeout double with this hand, because you have only two clubs. It is much better to overcall 1♠, showing a five-card suit. If you make a takeout double and your partner bids 2♣, he will be very disappointed in your trump support. By overcalling 1♠ at your first turn, you may still be in a position to bid your hearts later in the auction.

The third requirement refers to **dummy points**. When you make a takeout double, your hand will usually be put down as the dummy, so you count extra points for shortness in your RHO's opening bid suit, as follows: Void = 5, Singleton = 3, Doubleton = 1. Please note that **you do not count extra points for length** – once you give yourself extra points for shortness, you cannot count length points as well. Here are some examples of hands that qualify for a takeout double over your RHO's opening bid of 1♦:

HAND 1	HAND 2	HAND 3
♠ KT43	♠ KT43	♠ AQ43
♥ A974	♥ Q974	♥ A974
♦ 6	♦ ——	♦ 63
♣ K982	♣ K9832	♣ K52

Hand 1 has ten high card points, plus three points for the singleton diamond, so you should make a takeout double. Hand 2 has eight high card points, plus five for the diamond void, and should also make a takeout double. Notice that you do not have enough points to open the bidding with either Hand 1 or Hand 2, but your excellent distribution enables you to make a takeout double over a 1♦ opening on your right. Hand 3 has thirteen high card points, plus one for the doubleton diamond, and should make a takeout double. Notice that **the less distribution you have, the more high card points you need to make a takeout double.**

It is perfectly acceptable to make a takeout double holding a five-card minor suit, but you should prefer to overcall in a five-card major suit rather than make a takeout double. Making a takeout double with a five-card major is losing tactics because you lose the ability to play in a 5-3 fit. For example, your RHO opens 1♦, and you hold:

♠ AQ7
♥ KJ943
♦ 62
♣ KQ5

If you make a takeout double with this hand, your partner is not going to bid a three-card heart suit. Your partner will probably respond in spades if he has a four-card spade suit, and you will wind up playing in a 4-3 spade fit instead of a 5-3 heart fit whenever your partner has three hearts.

Making offshape takeout doubles leads to more poor results than any other bid. Just remember the basic operating principle: **Whenever you have length in your RHO's suit, pass or overcall 1NT.**

If you pass because you have length and strength in your RHO's suit, you do not necessarily have to pass for the remainder of the auction. Sometimes you are able to make a delayed takeout double. For example, you hold:

♠ A987
♥ 7
♦ AQT7
♣ KQT8

If your RHO opens 1♣, 1♦, or 1♠, you must pass, since your hand is unsuitable for either a takeout double or a 1NT overcall. Suppose the auction proceeds as follows:

RHO	YOU	LHO	PARTNER
1♣	Pass	1♥	Pass
2♥	?		

Once the opponents have bid and raised hearts, you can now come into the auction with a takeout double. This shows heart shortness and support for each of the other three suits, including clubs. If your partner has length in clubs, he should bid 3♣ over your takeout double, knowing that you promise length in clubs for your delayed takeout double.

You should strive to avoid making a takeout double when you have length in the opponent's suit. This is the cause of many bridge disasters. Here is an illustrative example:

DLR: East   ♠ Q63
VUL: Both   ♥ AJT954
Rubber Bridge   ♦ 53
                ♣ 54

♠ JT52		♠ K4
♥ 832		♥ KQ6
♦ K2		♦ J9864
♣ 9762		♣ AJ3

              ♠ A987
              ♥ 7
              ♦ AQT7
              ♣ KQT8

When east opened the bidding 1♦, south could not bear to pass with fifteen points, and said double. Partner naturally jumped to 4♥, which went down two tricks. Here is how the auction should have gone:

South	West	North	East
			1♦
Pass	Pass	1♥	Pass
1NT	Pass	2♥	All Pass

There are two good reasons for south to bid just 1NT over his partner's 1♥ balancing bid: 1) Partner does not need much to balance at the one-level, and is limited to less than an opening hand; 2) The hand is known to be a misfit, and when the hands are a misfit, you should keep the bidding low.

Suppose that over your RHO's 1♦ opening, everyone passed. Would it be so terrible to defend 1♦ with AQT7 in their suit? You will never get a zero for getting a plus score on this type of hand.

Suppose you hold: ♠ AKJ6
                          ♥ 6
                          ♦ AQJ985
                          ♣ 85

If your RHO opens 1♥, do not make an offshape takeout double with only two clubs. You should overcall 2♦, willing to bid spades at your next opportunity to show a strong offensive hand. This is a better description of this hand than doubling and then bidding diamonds over a 2♣ response.

Occasionally, your RHO will open the bidding at the one-level, and you have a hand that is **too strong to overcall at the one-level** (remember that a one-level overcall is limited to a maximum of 17 points). The solution to this problem is to **double and then bid your own suit, or double and then bid notrump** to show a hand that is too strong to take action at the one-level. Once you bid your own suit over partner's response to your takeout double, you negate the message of the takeout double and show 18 or more points and a good five-card or longer suit. Here are some examples of hands that should double first and then bid a suit or notrump over your RHO's opening bid of 1♦:

<table>
<tr><td>HAND 1</td><td>HAND 2</td></tr>
<tr><td>♠ AQ</td><td>♠ AQ6</td></tr>
<tr><td>♥ AKT74</td><td>♥ AJ95</td></tr>
<tr><td>♦ 52</td><td>♦ AJ8</td></tr>
<tr><td>♣ KQ63</td><td>♣ A74</td></tr>
</table>

On Hand 1, you are too strong to simply overcall 1♥, so you make a takeout double. If your partner bids 1♠, you will bid 2♥ to show 18 or more points and at least five hearts.

On Hand 2, you are too strong to overcall 1NT. When you double first and then bid notrump, you are showing a balanced hand of 19-20 points, too strong to overcall 1NT. **These are the only hand types that can make a takeout double with length in the opponent's suit.**

Responding to Partner's Takeout Double

A. Suit Responses

Remember that your partner's takeout double is forcing for one round, and you must bid something if your RHO passes*. **The weaker your hand is, the more imperative it is for you to make a bid.** If you pass because you have a very weak hand, the predictable result is that the opponents will make their doubled contract with overtricks. Partner has asked you to bid your longest suit, and you should oblige him. Bidding a new suit at a minimum level does not show any highcard points – partner has forced you to bid no matter how weak your hand is.

Responder's point ranges for responding in a new suit are as follows:

0 to 8 points: Bid a new suit at a minimum level
9 to 11 points: Jump one level in a new suit
12+ points: Jump to game, or **cuebid the opponent's suit** if you are not sure of what game to bid. This is either a choice of games cuebid or the start of a slam inquiry

* On rare occasions, you may pass your partner's takeout double at the one-level with an excellent holding in their suit. If you pass a low-level takeout double, partner is expected to **lead trumps**.

B. Notrump Responses

Partner has shown a three-suited hand with shortness in the opponent's suit and does not want to hear you respond in notrump. Therefore, bidding any number of notrump **shows a double stopper in the opponent's suit and constructive values.** Point ranges for notrump responses are as follows:

8 to 11 points: Bid 1NT
12 to 14 points: Jump to 2NT
15 to 17 points: Jump to 3NT

Here are some sample hands for you to bid over your partner's takeout double. In each case, the auction has proceeded as follows:

LHO	Partner	RHO	You
1♠	DBL	Pass	?

HAND 1	HAND 2	HAND 3
♠ QT843	♠ A6	♠ 865
♥ 972	♥ Q9653	♥ T765432
♦ 65	♦ K85	♦ A
♣ 975	♣ J62	♣ 42

HAND 4	HAND 5	HAND 6
♠ 732	♠ 53	♠ AQ53
♥ KQJ764	♥ Q943	♥ QT7
♦ A	♦ 4	♦ JT
♣ K64	♣ KJ8652	♣ 8654

ANSWERS

1. **Bid 2♣** – You have the worst possible hand you could have, but partner has forced you to bid. Passing partner's takeout double will result in the opponents making 1♠ doubled with overtricks. Bid your cheapest three-card suit.

2. **Jump to 3♥** – You want to invite a game in hearts. You would make this same bid with four hearts, since partner tends to have four-card support.

3. **Jump to 4♥** – Your side has at least ten hearts (your partner's takeout double promised at least three-card support), so follow the **Law of Total Trumps** and let the opponents guess what to do at a high level.

4. **Cuebid 2♠** – You are interested in a slam in hearts, so start out with a forcing bid by cuebidding 2♠.

5. **Bid 2♣** – You have a maximum non-jump response. If you only had five clubs, you should bid 2♥ instead. It is generally better to respond in a four-card major rather than a five-card minor over partner's takeout double.

6. **Bid 1NT** – This shows 8 to 11 points and a double spade stopper.

Sometimes, when you are responding to your partner's takeout double, you must plan ahead as to how the rest of the auction might proceed. For example, your LHO opens 1♣, your partner makes a takeout double, and you hold:

♠ K652
♥ KQ85
♦ 94
♣ 972

You should respond 1♠ rather than 1♥. Do not bid four-card major suits up the line in response to your partner's takeout double, because you will be ill prepared for further bids if the opponents compete further. For example, suppose the auction proceeds:

LHO	Partner	RHO	You
1♣	DBL	Pass	1♥
2♣	Pass	Pass	?

If you want to bid your spade suit and your partner likes hearts better, **you force your partner to bid 3♥** to go back to your first bid suit. By bidding spades first, you can bid 2♥ if the opponents compete further, and **your partner will be able to take a preference at the two-level.**

C. Bidding Over the Opponent's Takeout Double

When your partner opens the bidding at the one-level and your RHO makes a takeout double, you are no longer required to respond with 6 or 7 points, since your partner will get another chance to bid. Similarly, it is no longer necessary to respond with a four-card major suit, since the takeout doubler has shown length in each of the unbid suits. It is perfectly acceptable to bid 1NT over your RHO's takeout double with one or even two four-card major suits if you have a balanced hand. The basic principles of bidding over your RHO's takeout double are as follows:

1) A new suit is forcing for one round at the one-level, but is **not forcing** at the two-level. Bidding a new suit should be somewhat lead-directional – do not bid a weak five-card suit that you do not want your partner to lead. Conversely, you should bid a good four-card suit over your RHO's takeout double if you want your partner to lead that suit.

2) A jump in a new suit is preemptive, showing a six-card or longer suit and less than eight points.

3) A jump in partner's suit is also preemptive, showing a fit for partner's suit and a weak hand.

4) A redouble shows ten or more points and creates a forcing auction – your side must either declare the hand or double the opponents in their contract. Not all hands containing ten or more points should redouble – with a two-suited hand and a fit in your partner's suit, you should bid a new suit at the one-level first.

5) A free bid of 1NT over your RHO's takeout double shows 8 to 10 points, and may contain one or two four-card majors.

Here are some sample hands for you to bid over your RHO's takeout double. In each case, the auction has proceeded as follows:

Partner	RHO	You
1 ♣	DBL	?

HAND 1	HAND 2	HAND 3	HAND 4
♠ KT85	♠ 832	♠ 3	♠ QJT974
♥ QJ76	♥ AKJ7	♥ AKT74	♥ 74
♦ K54	♦ 63	♦ 63	♦ J63
♣ 86	♣ 9743	♣ KJ743	♣ 86

ANSWERS

1. **Bid 1NT** – Since your RHO strongly suggested possession of both majors, there is no point in bidding either of your four-card major suits. Your free bid of 1NT promises 8 to 10 points and a balanced hand, and does not deny a four-card major suit.

2. **Bid 1♥** – Bid the suit you want your partner to lead.

3. **Bid 1♥** – You will jump in clubs at your next turn to set up a game-forcing auction. The problem with redoubling to show ten or more points is that an enterprising LHO will jump to 4♠ with spade length, and you will be faced with a nasty guess at your next turn whether to show your heart suit or raise your partner's clubs. Bidding 1♥ at your first turn eliminates this potential problem.

4. **Bid 2♠** – Over your RHO's takeout double, this is a weak bid and shows a six-card or longer suit.

For the next four hands, the auction has proceeded as follows:

Partner	RHO	You
1 ♥	DBL	?

HAND 5	HAND 6	HAND 7	HAND 8
♠ 83	♠ K4	♠ 3	♠ KT8
♥ J6	♥ QT84	♥ Q8754	♥ 83
♦ KQJ875	♦ K982	♦ 8632	♦ KJ42
♣ 762	♣ A54	♣ 762	♣ QT65

ANSWERS

5. **Bid 2♦** – This is a non-forcing bid, showing a six-card or longer suit and fewer than ten points.

6. **Redouble** – You will support hearts at your next turn. Some players use a convention called **Jordan**, where a jump to 2NT promises a limit raise or better with four-card support. If you play Jordan, this hand should jump to 2NT to show heart support and a good hand.

7. **Bid 3♥ or 4♥**, depending on vulnerability – You want to raise hearts preemptively over your RHO's takeout double.

8. **Bid 1NT** – This is a constructive bid, showing 8 to 10 points without a fit for your partner's suit.

Here are some examples of takeout doubles in the context of an entire hand:

DLR: East   ♠ QJ94
VUL: Both   ♥ KQ86
Matchpoints   ♦ A5
                   ♣ T94

   ♠ 763   ♠ K8
   ♥ J943   ♥ 72
   ♦ 842   ♦ J93
   ♣ J86   ♣ AKQ732

                   ♠ AT52
                   ♥ AT5
                   ♦ KQT76
                   ♣ 5

South	West	North	East
			1♣
DBL	Pass	2♣	DBL
2♦	Pass	2♥	Pass
2♠	Pass	4♠	All Pass

With two four-card majors and a game-forcing hand, north cuebids 2♣ to get to the right game. With diamonds breaking 3-3 and the king of spades onside, twelve tricks can be made in spades, but only eleven tricks are available in the 4-3 heart fit.

DLR: West   ♠ 4
VUL: N-S   ♥ QJ86
Matchpoints   ♦ AKJT5
              ♣ AQ2

♠ AQ9852   ♠ KT63
♥ 75   ♥ A3
♦ 76   ♦ 9832
♣ KJ5   ♣ T83

               ♠ J7
               ♥ KT942
               ♦ Q4
               ♣ 9764

South	West	North	East
	2♠	DBL	4♠
Pass	Pass	DBL	Pass
5♥	All Pass		

North makes a takeout double over the weak 2♠ opening bid, and south is not strong enough to take a free bid over east's jump to 4♠. North now doubles again, **showing a takeout double with extra values**, and south now bids 5♥, which makes eleven tricks with a successful club finesse.

DLR: North
VUL: E-W
Matchpoints

♠ QJ86
♥ 32
♦ AKJ7
♣ AQ7

♠ A42
♥ 97
♦ 96
♣ KJ9543

♠ K5
♥ AKJT86
♦ T843
♣ 6

♠ T973
♥ Q54
♦ Q52
♣ T82

North	East	South	West
1NT	2♥	Pass	Pass
DBL	Pass	2♠	All Pass

If you open the bidding and your LHO bids a suit and the bidding comes back to you, you can make a **reopening double**. A reopening double is the same as a takeout double, except that you have already opened the bidding. On this hand, north wants to compete over 2♥, so he reopens with double, asking partner to bid his longest suit. Remember that doubling when the bidder is on your left is for takeout; if the bidder were on the right of the notrump opener, the double would be for penalties. On this hand, south makes nine tricks in spades, and the opponents would have made eight tricks in hearts.

We have seen that if you make a takeout double and the opponents bid further and your partner passes, making a second double is a repeat takeout double with extra values. How about if your partner bids a suit and the opponents compete further? What does a second double by the original takeout doubler show?

In order to answer this question, we have to go back to the basic principle that **the nature of a double never changes:** If the first double was a takeout double, the second double is a repeat takeout double with extra values. Why would you make a repeat takeout double when you can simply raise your partner's suit? The answer is that **you have extra values and only three-card support for partner's suit.** Your second double asks partner to do something intelligent, knowing that you have just three-card support. Here is an example of a hand that would make a repeat takeout double after the opponents compete further:

> ♠ AK85
> ♥ AQ7
> ♦ 7
> ♣ KJ763

Your RHO opens 1♦, you double, your LHO passes, and your partner responds 1♥. If your RHO rebids 2♦, you must double again to show this hand. If you had a fourth heart, you would freely raise hearts rather than double again.

KEY POINTS

1. The nature of a double never changes. If the first double was negative, responsive or takeout, the second double shows the same type of double with **extra values**.

2. Whenever the opponents have bid and raised the same suit, all doubles are for takeout. The higher the bidding level, the likelier it is that your partner will convert it into penalties by passing, but partner should bid with a long suit and some values.

3. A negative double applies when your partner opens a suit at the one-level and your RHO overcalls in a new suit. It is a convenient way to show values when you do not meet the requirements needed to bid a new suit. Negative doubles tend to show four or more cards in any unbid major, but this is not a guarantee.

4. When you open the bidding, your LHO overcalls in a new suit, and there are two passes to you, strain to make a reopening double whenever you are short in the opponent's suit.

5. A responsive double is a way of showing values when the opponents have bid and raised the same suit after your partner has either overcalled or made a takeout double. Just as with negative doubles, the higher the level that the opponents compete to, the more points you need to make a responsive double.

6. A cooperative double is a way to show values when the opponents compete in the auction. It shows values with no clearcut bid to make and asks partner to do something intelligent. Cooperative doubles also apply when you

jump to game over your RHO's opening bid with a good hand, and the opponents compete further.

7. A takeout double applies when your RHO opens the bidding with a suit bid. In order to make a takeout double, you need shortness in the opponent's suit, at least three-card support for each of the unbid suits, and thirteen or more points including dummy points. In addition, the hand should generally not contain a five-card major suit.

8. When your partner makes a takeout double, you must respond unless you have a strong holding in the opponent's suit. Bidding a new suit without jumping does not show any points at all. You are simply bidding your longest suit, as your partner requested you to do.

9. If your RHO makes a takeout double, a free bid of 1NT shows eight to ten points and may contain one or two four-card major suits. You can redouble with ten or more points, and bidding a new suit is forcing at the one-level but non-forcing at the two level. All jumps by an unpassed hand are weak, since you would redouble if you had ten or more points. Jumps by a passed hand are **fit-showing jumps**, even over the opponent's takeout double.

BIDDING QUIZ

1. None Vulnerable, you hold:

	Partner	RHO	You
♠ 76	1♦	1♠	?
♥ KJ9765			
♦ Q96			
♣ Q64			

2. Both Vulnerable, you hold:

	You	LHO	Partner	RHO
♠ AQ976	1♠	2♣	Pass	Pass
♥ KJ87	?			
♦ K92				
♣ 4				

3. Non-vulnerable versus Vulnerable, you hold:

	LHO	Partner	RHO	You
♠ QT76	1♦	DBL	3♦*	?
♥ KJ53				
♦ 976				
♣ K7			* Preemptive	

4. Vulnerable versus non-vulnerable, you hold:

♠ 754	Partner	RHO	You	LHO
♥ JT	1♥	Pass	1NT*	2♠
♦ K875	Pass	Pass	?	
♣ AJT6			* Forcing	

5. Both Vulnerable, you hold:

♠ KT86	RHO	You
♥ ——	1♥	?
♦ K973		
♣ KJ742		

6. None Vulnerable, you hold:

♠ KT86	LHO	Partner	RHO	You
♥ QT73	1♦	DBL	Pass	?
♦ T5				
♣ Q52				

ANSWERS

1. **Make a negative double.** You intend to bid hearts at your next turn to show a five-card or longer heart suit without enough points to freely bid hearts at the two-level. Note that making a negative double and bidding a suit is weaker than bidding the suit directly.

2. **Make a reopening double**, showing shortness in the opponent's suit and at least three cards in each of the unbid suits. Note that your reopening double does not show extra values, it simply shows shortness in the opponent's suit. Your bid caters to partner having a trump stack, in which case he will convert your double to penalties by passing over your reopening double.

3. **Make a responsive double**, showing values and both major suits. Why guess which major suit to bid when you can enlist partner's cooperation in bidding your longest combined major suit?

4. **Make a cooperative double**, telling partner that your side has the majority of the points and asking your partner to make an intelligent decision.

5. **Make a takeout double.** Although you wouldn't have opened the bidding with this hand, your ideal distribution mandates making a takeout double.

6. **Bid 1♠.** Do not bid major suits "up the line" when your partner makes a takeout double. This way, if the opponents compete further, you can bid 2♥ and let partner choose between hearts and spades at the two-level.

CHAPTER 6

DECLARER PLAY

A. Counting Points and Distribution

Whether you are the declarer or a defender, you must get accustomed to counting out the hand. Counting out the hand involves counting both the high card points and the distribution of the unseen hands. It is generally a good idea to add your points and the points in the dummy in order to get an idea of how many points are in each of the other two hands. This will assist you in declaring or defending the hand.

Each bid that your opponents make gives away information about their points and distribution. You should be paying attention to your opponents' auction so that you are able to take advantage of this information.

Here is an example of counting points:

```
DLR: East          ♠ 7654
VUL: E-W           ♥ 87
Rubber Bridge      ♦ K42
                   ♣ KJT3

♠ QT83                          ♠ AKJ
♥ 64                            ♥ A53
♦ 986                           ♦ QJT3
♣ A954                          ♣ Q87

                   ♠ 92
                   ♥ KQJT92
                   ♦ A75
                   ♣ 62
```

South	West	North	East
			1NT
2♥	All Pass		

South declares 2♥ after east has opened the bidding 1NT. As soon as dummy comes down, south should count points. Dummy has seven points and the declarer has ten points, leaving 23 points in the other two hands. The 1NT opener should have 16 points on average, leaving about seven points for west.

The opening lead of the three of spades is won by east's king, and east continues with the ace and jack of spades. Declarer trumps the third round of spades and knocks out the ace of hearts. East now shifts to the queen of diamonds, and declarer wins the ace and draws trump. Making the contract now depends on guessing the location of the missing club honors. So far, east, who opened 1NT, has shown up with the ace, king and jack of spades, the ace of hearts, and the queen and jack of diamonds, a total of fifteen points. If east held the ace of clubs as well, he would have nineteen points, **and would be too strong to open a 15- to 17-point notrump.**

Therefore, declarer should lead a club to the king and make the contract.

Here is another example of counting points:

DLR: South   ♠ 852
VUL: Both   ♥ Q752
Matchpoints   ♦ AK3
                        ♣ QT3

♠ KQJT3   ♠ A96
♥ A4   ♥ JT9
♦ 86   ♦ 9752
♣ J864   ♣ 975

                        ♠ 74
                        ♥ K863
                        ♦ QJT4
                        ♣ AK2

South	West	North	East
1 ♦	1 ♠	DBL	Pass
2 ♥	Pass	3 ♥	All Pass

South is the declarer in 3♥ after west has made a vulnerable 1♠ overcall. The defenders play three rounds of spades, declarer ruffing the third round. In counting points, declarer observes that the opponents have a combined total of 16 points. Once east shows up with the ace of spades, it is fair to assume that west will have the ace of trumps. Accordingly, declarer leads a low heart to dummy's queen. When the queen holds the trick, west is marked with the ace of hearts, and **the only way to lose just one trump trick is to duck a second round of trumps**, playing west for Ax of trumps. When this play works, declarer makes an overtrick. If west had three hearts, it wouldn't matter what the declarer does – he will lose two spades and two trump tricks, making 3♥.

Here is an excellent example of card reading:

DLR: West   ♠ KQ93
VUL: None   ♥ 952
Matchpoints ◆ J9
      ♣ QT63

♠ A542   ♠ T86
♥ KT   ♥ J87
◆ T8   ◆ A6542
♣ AJ972   ♣ K5

      ♠ J7
      ♥ AQ643
      ◆ KQ73
      ♣ 84

South	West	North	East
	1♣	Pass	1NT
2♥	All Pass		

On west's opening lead of the ten of diamonds, south should figure out the entire hand. The opponents have twenty points between them, with the opening bidder having about thirteen and the 1NT responder having about seven. The opening lead marks the 1NT responder with the ace of diamonds **and one of the two top club honors**, since west would have led a top club holding both the ace and the king. Therefore, west is marked with the king of hearts, and **declarer's only chance to make the hand is that west has the doubleton king of trumps**, since he has four losers outside of the trump suit. As the only chance, declarer must attack trumps by playing the ace and then a low trump. When west's king falls doubleton, declarer picks up the trump suit for one loser and makes the contract.

Sometimes, counting points will show that taking a normal finesse is guaranteed to fail, and the only way to make the hand is to take an **unusual finesse**. Here is a complete hand that illustrates this concept:

DLR: East
VUL: Both
Matchpoints

```
              ♠ T98
              ♥ K64
              ♦ AJ54
              ♣ KJ9
♠ 5                        ♠ K63
♥ JT953                    ♥ AQ7
♦ 973                      ♦ KQ82
♣ T872                     ♣ Q63
              ♠ AQJ742
              ♥ 82
              ♦ T6
              ♣ A54
```

South	West	North	East
			1NT
2♠	Pass	3♠	Pass
4♠	All Pass		

South declares 4♠ after east opens 1NT, and he receives the opening lead of the jack of hearts. In counting points, declarer sees twenty-three points between his hand and the dummy, **so the 1NT opener must have all of the missing points.** Declarer must lose two hearts and a diamond, so he must bring in spades and clubs for no losers in order to make the contract. Declarer can expect the spade finesse to work, but the club finesse is guaranteed to lose, since the 1NT opener is marked with the queen of clubs. Declarer's only chance to make the contract is to take a **backwards finesse** in clubs, leading the jack from dummy and capturing east's queen with his ace. Declarer now finesses west for the ten of clubs by leading a low club to dummy's nine – when this finesse succeeds, the contract rolls home.

Besides counting points, a good declarer needs to be able to count the distribution of the two defending hands. Here is an example of counting out the distribution, based on a hand by Eddie Kantar:

DLR: South   ♠ 632
VUL: None   ♥ 32
Matchpoints   ♦ JT65
             ♣ KT75

♠ QT84   ♠ J97
♥ A654   ♥ KT7
♦ 3   ♦ A9872
♣ J862   ♣ 94

             ♠ AK5
             ♥ QJ98
             ♦ KQ4
             ♣ AQ3

South	West	North	East
2NT	Pass	Pass	Pass

Declarer wins the opening lead of the four of spades with the king. Declarer now plays the king and queen of diamonds, knocking out east's ace, as west shows out on the second round, discarding a heart. When west shows out on the second round of diamonds, what is his distribution in the other three suits? West is marked with a 4-4-1-4 distribution, **since he would have led from a five-card suit if he had one**. Declarer knows that the four of spades was a fourth best lead, since he can see the three and the two in the dummy. Therefore, declarer cashes the ace and queen of clubs, and if the jack does not fall, confidently finesses the ten of clubs on the third round. This results in nine tricks – two spades, three diamonds, and four clubs.

Whenever the opponents make a preemptive bid, they reveal a great deal of information about their distribution, and a good declarer will make good use of this information. Here is an example of making use of the information obtained from the opponent's preemptive bid:

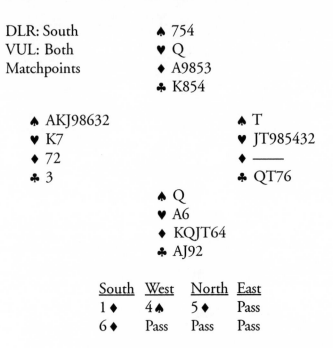

DLR: South
VUL: Both
Matchpoints

♠ 754
♥ Q
♦ A9853
♣ K854

♠ AKJ98632
♥ K7
♦ 72
♣ 3

♠ T
♥ JT985432
♦ ——
♣ QT76

♠ Q
♥ A6
♦ KQJT64
♣ AJ92

South	West	North	East
1♦	4♠	5♦	Pass
6♦	Pass	Pass	Pass

West leads the ace and king of spades, as east shows out on the second round and declarer ruffs. Declarer draws trump in two rounds, east showing out on the first round, and plays ace of hearts and ruffs a heart in dummy, west following to both rounds. West is marked with eight spades, two hearts, two diamonds, **and therefore has only one club.** Declarer therefore plays the king of clubs and leads a second round, finessing the nine when east plays low. It is now a simple matter to get back to dummy with a trump and repeat the marked club finesse to make the slam.

B. Combining Chances

An expert bridge player is very reluctant to stake the fate of the contract on a finesse. He is always looking for an extra chance to make the hand should the finesse fail. Here is an example of combining chances:

Dummy	Declarer
♠ AJ3	♠ K82
♥ AT9853	♥ KJ72
♦ AK	♦ 843
♣ Q2	♣ A85

Suppose you get to 6♥ with these two hands, and you receive the opening lead of the queen of diamonds. You win the first trick in dummy perforce, and you draw trumps, which break 2-1. How do you play the hand?

Obviously, you will make the slam whenever the spade finesse works. Can you see another chance to make the slam when the spade finesse is wrong?

Before you play a spade, **you should lead a low club from your hand towards the dummy.** Whenever the king of clubs sits in front of the king, that player will have to take his king, and you will eventually pitch a spade from dummy on your ace of clubs to make the slam without the spade finesse. Of course, if the queen of clubs loses to the king, you will have to fall back on the finesse.

Here is another example of combining chances:

Dummy	Declarer
♠ 8763	♠ AKQJ92
♥ 986	♥ KQ
♦ J4	♦ AQ
♣ AKQ3	♣ 862

Suppose you get to 6♠, and the opponents lead the ace of hearts and another heart. After you draw trumps, you see that you have two chances to make the slam: either the diamond finesse, or clubs dividing 3-3. Although a 3-3 club division is against the odds, **you must play on clubs first** to give yourself an extra chance. If clubs break 3-3, you can pitch your losing diamond away on the thirteenth club; if clubs are not 3-3, you can always take the diamond finesse later.

Suppose you get to 3NT with the following hands:

Dummy	Declarer
♠ K4	♠ 763
♥ Q542	♥ AK3
♦ KQT2	♦ A4
♣ JT5	♣ AQ943

The opening lead is a low spade, and you play dummy's king, which holds the trick. You have eight top tricks, with three chances for a ninth trick: 1) 3-3 hearts; 2) the jack of diamonds dropping on the third round; and 3) a successful club finesse. In order to combine your chances, you should try options (1) and (2) first, because if either of these two chances work, you will have nine tricks without giving up the lead. If you try the club finesse and it loses, the opponents will cash enough spade tricks to defeat your contract.

Try your skill at combining chances with another slam hand:

Dummy	Declarer
♠ QJ63	♠ ——
♥ 953	♥ AKQ2
♦ 52	♦ AKQJ9743
♣ J876	♣ 5

You get to 6♦, and the opponents cash the ace of clubs at trick one and continue with a high club. Anyone can make the slam when hearts divide 3-3, but can you make the slam against the normal 4-2 heart split?

The way to combine chances on this hand is to cash one high trump before playing the top three hearts. This enables you to make the slam not only when hearts are 3-3, **but also when hearts are 4-2 and the hand with four hearts has the last remaining trump.** In that case, he will have to follow suit as you ruff your heart loser with dummy's remaining trump.

Here is an example of combining chances in the context of a complete hand:

DLR: South
VUL: E-W
Rubber Bridge

	♠ 7		
	♥ KQJ4		
	♦ T8732		
	♣ AQ5		

♠ KJ842   ♠ Q9653
♥ T872   ♥ A653
♦ 4   ♦ Q
♣ JT9   ♣ K86

♠ AT
♥ 9
♦ AKJ965
♣ 7432

South	West	North	East
1 ♦	Pass	1 ♥	1 ♠
2 ♦	4 ♠	5 ♦	All Pass

On the sound reasoning that his side is not going to take more than one spade trick, west leads the jack of clubs against the 5 ♦ contract. In order to give himself an extra chance, **declarer must reject the club finesse and rise with dummy's ace.** If the club finesse would have worked, it will still work later. The problem with taking an immediate club finesse is that if it loses, the defenders will continue clubs and establish two clubs and one heart trick to set the contract. The extra chance from winning the ace of clubs at trick one comes in whenever east has the ace of hearts. After drawing trumps, declarer knocks out the ace of hearts, and if east wins it, he cannot attack clubs without giving up a trick to the queen. If east doesn't play clubs, declarer can pitch two clubs from his hand on the good hearts, losing one club and one heart. If west wins the ace of hearts, declarer is forced to take the club finesse **as a last-resort play.**

Sometimes you have to see what happens in one suit to determine your play in another suit, as the following hand illustrates:

DLR: South	♠ Q873	
VUL: N-S	♥ T963	
Swiss Teams	♦ AQ	
	♣ QJ7	

♠ ——		♠ KJ9
♥ 874		♥ K52
♦ JT986		♦ K5432
♣ T9862		♣ 43

♠ AT6542	
♥ AQJ	
♦ 7	
♣ AK5	

South	West	North	East
1 ♠	Pass	3 ♠	Pass
4NT	Pass	5 ♦	Pass
6 ♠	Pass	Pass	Pass

Declarer wins the opening jack of diamonds lead with dummy's ace, and needs to lose just one trick in the major suits to make the slam. If the heart finesse loses, declarer needs to pick up trumps for no losers, and his best play would be to lay down the ace of trumps, hoping for the king to fall singleton. However, if the heart finesse works, declarer can afford to take a **safety play** in trumps by leading low from his hand towards dummy's queen — this prevents the loss of two trump tricks when trumps are 3-0, as they are on this hand. Therefore, declarer takes the heart finesse at trick two. When the finesse succeeds, declarer makes the safety play in trumps and only loses one trump trick, making the slam.

C. Deception

In order to be a successful declarer, you need to develop a deceptive style. Your goal is to conceal your assets from the defenders, who are trying to count out your hand. There are certain well-known positions in which you must play a certain honor card in order to deceive the opponents. One position is as follows:

Dummy	Declarer
765	AK3

If you are declaring notrump and the opponents lead this suit, it is much more deceptive to win with the king than to win with the ace. If you had A32 opposite dummy's 765, you would hold up your ace until the third round, so you are not fooling anyone when you win the trick with the ace — the defenders should realize that you also hold the king, or else you would have held up. However, if you held K32 opposite 765, you would have to win the king at trick one, or you might never get a trick in this suit. Therefore, winning with the king keeps the opponents in the dark as to who holds the ace of that suit. Let us look at this position with two hands in view:

Dummy	Declarer
♠ 965	♠ AKJ
♥ Q83	♥ 765
♦ A9743	♦ K8
♣ A9	♣ KQ862

Suppose you are the declarer in 3NT, and you get a low spade opening lead to your RHO's queen. The best play at IMP's or Rubber Bridge is to win the first trick with the king, and take a first round finesse of the nine of clubs. If this finesse loses, your RHO would have to be a genius to switch to a heart at trick three. What is most likely to happen is that your RHO will play another spade, and you will take nine tricks - three spades, two diamonds and four clubs - without the opponents ever playing hearts, their best suit.

Sometimes you can induce the opponents to play a suit that you would rather not play yourself through deceptive play. For example:

Dummy	Declarer
♠ K2	♠ QJ3
♥ Q943	♥ AT876
♦ AJ762	♦ K4
♣ A9	♣ 653

You are the declarer in 4♥, and you get the opening lead of the king of clubs. After winning the ace, you should lead dummy's king of spades. Although you do not need to ruff spades in dummy, **your opponents do not know that.** After cashing their club trick, the opponents are quite likely to lead trumps to prevent spade ruffs in dummy, and you will be able to hold your trumps to one loser without having to guess the trump position.

For the next example, let us revert to showing all four hands:

```
DLR: South        ♠ A9654
VUL: Both         ♥ J
Matchpoints       ♦ AQ53
                  ♣ J96

♠ ——                        ♠ K73
♥ K975                      ♥ Q862
♦ J42                       ♦ T9876
♣ AKT875                    ♣ 2

                  ♠ QJT82
                  ♥ AT43
                  ♦ K
                  ♣ Q43
```

South	West	North	East
1♠	2♣	3♣	Pass
3♠	Pass	4♠	All Pass

West leads the ace of clubs against south's 4♠ contract, and when east follows suit with the two, **south should realize that the two is singleton.** West must have at least five clubs for his 2♣ overcall, and east would high-low with a doubleton club, so therefore the two is a singleton. In order to deflect west from the winning action of continuing with the king of clubs and giving his partner a club ruff, **south must drop the queen of clubs under the ace at trick one.** If west believes that south is the one with the singleton club, he will shift to another suit for fear of setting up dummy's jack of clubs. Declarer can now unblock the king of diamonds, get to dummy with the ace of trumps, and pitch his two losing clubs on dummy's ace and queen of diamonds, and make an overtrick.

Needless to say, you must play your queen of clubs in tempo at trick one. If you think about it for a while and then drop the queen, the deception will not work, and the opponents will know what to do against you.

Sometimes, the opponents make the wrong opening lead against you — for example, defending against your notrump contract, they lead your long suit. If you want them to continue this suit, you must falsecard effectively. For example:

Dummy	Declarer
♠ KT94	♠ AQJ
♥ KJ63	♥ A72
♦ 752	♦ A4
♣ J9	♣ QT832

You open 1NT, and after a Stayman sequence, you become declarer in 3NT. You receive the opening lead of the four of clubs, which RHO wins with the king. **You must follow suit to this trick with the eight or the ten** in order to induce the opponents to continue clubs. If you follow with either the two or the three, your RHO will realize that you have five clubs, and will find the killing switch to a diamond. By playing a high spot card, your RHO may think that his partner led from a five-card club suit, and will continue clubs, enabling you to make 3NT with overtricks.

Deception is not limited to the declarer. The defenders can also indulge in a bit of deception when the occasion arises. A good time to make a deceptive opening lead is when fooling your partner won't matter because he has no high card points. For example:

DLR: North   ♠ K74
VUL: E-W   ♥ AKJ75
Rubber Bridge   ♦ T72
               ♣ Q6

```
        ♠ K74
        ♥ AKJ75
        ♦ T72
        ♣ Q6
♠ T95              ♠ J863
♥ Q93              ♥ T64
♦ AK953            ♦ 84
♣ A4               ♣ 9752
        ♠ AQ2
        ♥ 82
        ♦ QJ6
        ♣ KJT83
```

North	East	South	West
1♥	Pass	2NT	Pass
3NT	Pass	Pass	Pass

Natural bidding led to a normal 3NT contract. West realized that his partner had at most two points on this auction, so he made the deceptive lead of the **three of diamonds** from a five-card suit. Upon winning the diamond trick, declarer assumed that diamonds divided 4-3, and he had a cinch for his contract by knocking out the ace of clubs. Taking the heart finesse could result in going down in a cold contract – the defenders could take one heart, one club, and three diamonds. Declarer therefore played on clubs at trick two, and west took his ace of clubs and four diamond tricks to defeat the contract.

A good principle to follow is **to play the card that you are known, or will be known, to hold.** A defender followed this principle on the following hand, and received a matchpoint top for his efforts:

```
DLR: South          ♠ J32
VUL: N-S            ♥ Q8
Matchpoints         ♦ T9
                    ♣ AKJ763

    ♠ T4                        ♠ K863
    ♥ J9632                     ♥ A74
    ♦ J432                      ♦ Q86
    ♣ QT                        ♣ 842

                    ♠ AQ97
                    ♥ KT5
                    ♦ AK75
                    ♣ 95
```

South	West	North	East
1NT	Pass	3NT	All Pass

The opening lead of the three of hearts went to east's ace, and a heart was continued to dummy's queen. The jack of spades was covered by the king and ace, and declarer led a low club to dummy. West saw that his queen was a dead duck, so he tried the effect of playing the queen right away. This gave declarer a problem – if the queen was a singleton, then east had four clubs to the ten, and declarer needed to duck a club in order to run the club suit. Declarer therefore ducked the club trick and made only eleven tricks when the rest of the room was making twelve.

D. Restricted Choice

Suppose this is your trump suit:

You	Dummy
AKT62	9853

You lead the ace of trumps, and the queen drops on your left.

Do you play for the drop, or do you get to dummy in another suit and finesse your RHO for the jack of trumps?

According to the **Theory of Restricted Choice** (TRC), finessing your RHO for the jack of trumps is superior to playing for the drop. Let us see why this is true:

	LHO Plays	
LHO Holds	Queen of Trumps	Jack of Trumps
Q-J doubleton	50% of the time	50% of the time
Q singleton	100% of the time	———
J singleton	———	100% of the time

This table demonstrates that when LHO holds a singleton honor, his choice is **restricted** and the honor **must** be played; when LHO holds Q-J doubleton, he will play the queen 50% of the time and the jack 50% of the time. Therefore, when you lead the ace of trumps and LHO plays an honor, let us say the queen, it is more likely that LHO holds the singleton queen, **in which case the queen must be played**, than that LHO holds the Q-J doubleton, in which case the queen would be played only 50% of the time.

Let us see how TRC operates in the context of an entire hand:

DLR: South   ♠ T43
VUL: None   ♥ 98
Matchpoints   ♦ T965
             ♣ AK87

♠ J   ♠ Q72
♥ A72   ♥ QJ6543
♦ QJ87   ♦ K
♣ QT642   ♣ J53

             ♠ AK9865
             ♥ KT
             ♦ A432
             ♣ 9

South	West	North	East
1 ♠	Pass	2 ♠	Pass
4 ♠	All Pass		

West led the queen of diamonds, which was covered by east's king and declarer's ace. Declarer now cashed the ace of spades, noting the fall of the jack on his left. West's trump holding was either Q-J doubleton or the singleton jack, and the Theory of Restricted Choice made the latter holding more likely. Declarer led a club to the ace and pitched a heart on the king of clubs. The ten of spades was led from dummy, and when east played low, **declarer also played low, finessing east for the queen of trumps.** When the ten of spades held the trick, declarer drew trumps, played a low diamond to dummy, and eventually made eleven tricks, losing just one diamond and one heart.

Here is another hand which demonstrates TRC:

DLR: South   ♠ A
VUL: N-S   ♥ A942
Matchpoints   ♦ A752
                ♣ T853

♠ KQJ8763   ♠ 95
♥ T6   ♥ KQ873
♦ T93   ♦ 6
♣ J   ♣ Q7642

            ♠ T42
            ♥ J5
            ♦ KQJ84
            ♣ AK9

South	West	North	East
1 ♦	3 ♠	4 ♠	Pass
5 ♣	Pass	5 ♥	Pass
6 ♦	Pass	Pass	Pass

Declarer used TRC to make the slam. The king of spades opening lead was won in dummy, followed by the ace of diamonds and a diamond to declarer's king. Surprisingly, east showed out on the second round, leaving west with ten cards in spades and diamonds. A second spade was ruffed in dummy, followed by a trump to declarer's queen. Declarer now made the key play of cashing the ace of clubs, noting the fall of the jack of clubs on his left. Declarer ruffed his last spade in dummy and ran the ten of clubs, using TRC. When the ten of clubs held the trick, declarer repeated the club finesse and conceded a heart trick at the end to make the slam.

Here is another spectacular example of TRC:

DLR: South	♠ A4
VUL: Both	♥ T754
Matchpoints	♦ AT3
	♣ AK92

♠ QT863		♠ KJ975
♥ J6		♥ 8
♦ J6		♦ KQ542
♣ T854		♣ J3

	♠ 2
	♥ AKQ983
	♦ 987
	♣ Q76

South	West	North	East
1♥	Pass	2NT*	Pass
4♥	Pass	4NT	Pass
5♠**	Pass	6♥	All Pass

*Forcing heart raise ** 2 keycards and the trump queen

Declarer won the opening spade lead, drew trumps, and had to figure out a way to avoid losing two diamond tricks. Declarer played a club to the ace and a low club back to his queen, noting the fall of the jack on his right. Using restricted choice principles, he led his third club and **finessed the nine**. When the nine of clubs held, declarer pitched a diamond on the king of clubs and made the slam.

E. Loser on Loser Play

When you are the declarer in a suit contract and your RHO leads a suit that you are void in, you would normally trump it. However, there are many situations in which trumping would result in going down in your contract. The first situation involves **losing control** in the trump suit. Here is an illustrative hand:

```
DLR: North              ♠ T43
VUL: N-S                ♥ KT6
Rubber Bridge           ♦ 65
                        ♣ AKQ43

  ♠ AKQ97                            ♠ J85
  ♥ 8743                             ♥ 95
  ♦ QJ7                              ♦ KT83
  ♣ 86                               ♣ 975

                        ♠ 62
                        ♥ AQJ2
                        ♦ A942
                        ♣ JT2
```

North	East	South	West
1♣	Pass	1♥	1♠
2♥	Pass	4♥	All Pass

West plays three rounds of spades, and on the third round of spades, declarer is able to trump it. Let us see what happens if declarer trumps the third round.

If declarer trumps the third spade, declarer must draw trumps in order to run the clubs. Declarer can draw three rounds of trumps, but west remains with the thirteenth trump. When declarer tries running the clubs, west ruffs the third round and cashes two spade tricks, since the declarer is out of trumps. Declarer will eventually lose a diamond trick to go down three tricks.

Now let us see what happens when declarer properly discards a diamond loser on the third round of spades. Dummy is now void in spades, so if the defenders persist with a fourth spade, dummy can ruff, while declarer remains with four trumps. If the defenders shift to diamonds (best defense), declarer wins the ace of diamonds, draws trumps in four rounds, and runs dummy's club suit, pitching his remaining two diamond losers on dummy's good clubs.

A second situation where a loser on loser play is appropriate is **in order to avoid an enemy trump promotion**. This situation occurs when both you (declarer) and your LHO are void in a suit that your RHO leads. If you ruff with a high trump, your LHO pitches a loser and eventually scores a trump trick; if you ruff low, your LHO overruffs. By pitching a loser instead of ruffing, you can frequently avoid losing a trump trick. Here is an example hand:

DLR: South	♠ A742		
VUL: E-W	♥ T7432		
Matchpoints	♦ Q4		
	♣ AQ		

♠ QT9		♠ 865
♥ 5		♥ J86
♦ AKJT65		♦ 82
♣ T43		♣ 98765

	♠ KJ3
	♥ AKQ9
	♦ 973
	♣ KJ2

South	West	North	East
1NT	2♦	3♦*	Pass
3♥	Pass	4♥	All Pass

* Stayman

West led the ace and king of diamonds and continued with the jack of diamonds when east played high-low to show a doubleton. If declarer ruffs this trick high with dummy's ten of hearts, east will overruff, and declarer will eventually go down one when the spade finesse fails. However, declarer made a **loser on loser** play by pitching a spade from dummy on the third round of diamonds. Now declarer was able to draw trumps, pitch another spade from dummy on his third high club, and claim.

Even a strong trump holding can fall prey to an enemy trump promotion, as the following hand illustrates:

DLR: South   ♠ K7
VUL: None   ♥ J92
Matchpoints   ♦ KJ842
               ♣ AT7

♠ T854   ♠ 2
♥ K4   ♥ AQT753
♦ 96   ♦ QT5
♣ J9852   ♣ Q64

             ♠ AQJ963
             ♥ 86
             ♦ A73
             ♣ K3

South	West	North	East
1♠	Pass	2♦	2♥
2♠	Pass	4♠	All Pass

West led the king of hearts and the four of hearts to his partner's queen. When east continues with the ace of hearts, **declarer must not ruff this trick**. If declarer ruffs the third heart high, west pitches a card in a side suit, and the defenders eventually come to a trump trick and a diamond trick. If the declarer ruffs this trick with a low trump, west can overruff and exit passively with a trump. The defenders will eventually score a diamond for the setting trick. Instead, declarer makes a **loser on loser** play by pitching a diamond, and the defenders cannot take another trick.

Here is a spectacular example of a loser on loser play:

DLR: South	♠ 72	
VUL: N-S	♥ JT9852	
Matchpoints	♦ 72	
	♣ K83	

♠ 65		♠ T983
♥ K6		♥ Q73
♦ KQJT65		♦ A984
♣ QT6		♣ 74

	♠ AKQJ4	
	♥ A4	
	♦ 3	
	♣ AJ952	

South	West	North	East
1♠	2♦	Pass	3♦
4♣	Pass	4♠	All Pass

The defenders started out with two rounds of diamonds against 4♠, and declarer was at the crossroads at trick two. Declarer is missing six trumps, which will normally break 4-2. If declarer trumps the second diamond trick, he needs to use the rest of his trumps to draw all of the opponents' trumps, and he is now dependent on the club finesse. If the club finesse fails, the defenders can cash all of their diamonds, since declarer is out of trumps. The winning play is to throw away the inevitable heart loser at trick two. Dummy's trumps protect declarer against a further force in diamonds, and on any other return, declarer can win, draw four rounds of trumps, and take a club finesse. When this finesse loses, declarer has another trump to prevent the run of the diamonds, and makes his contract.

When a suit is led in which dummy has a void, it may be better to discard a loser from dummy instead of ruffing, if this will set up an eventual winner in declarer's hand. In this way, a second loser can be discarded from the dummy on the established winner in declarer's hand. If declarer's holding is Kxx or even QJxx, declarer can frequently gain an extra trick by discarding a loser from the dummy rather than ruffing. Here is an example hand:

DLR: East
VUL: Both
Matchpoints

	♠ AT932	
	♥	
	♦ 764	
	♣ AJ975	

♠ 8		♠ 75
♥ J86		♥ AQT953
♦ Q932		♦ KJ5
♣ KQ862		♣ T3

	♠ KQJ64	
	♥ K742	
	♦ AT8	
	♣ 4	

East	South	West	North
1♥	1♠	2♥	4♥*
Pass	4♠	Pass	5♣
Pass	6♠	All Pass	

* Splinter in support of spades

If declarer ruffs the opening heart lead in dummy, he risks losing two diamond tricks and going down in his slam if the fifth club in dummy cannot be established as a winner. The chances of a 4-3 club break are 62%, but relying on the club suit would fail on the actual lie of the cards.

Declarer has a sure way to make twelve tricks **by simply discarding a diamond loser from dummy at trick one.** East wins the heart ace, but declarer's king of hearts is now a winner, enabling declarer to discard a second diamond loser from dummy. Declarer draws trumps and ruffs two diamonds in dummy, making the slam. On a non-heart opening lead, declarer would have no chance to make the slam.

F. <u>Playing In A 4-3 Fit</u>

The main advantage of playing in a 4-3 trump fit is the ability to score an extra trick by ruffing a loser in the short trump hand. Trump strength is of primary importance, particularly in the four-card holding.

A 4-3 fit is often chosen because one suit is inadequately stopped for notrump. The time that it is right to play in a 4-3 fit is **when you can do the ruffing in the short trump hand,** keeping the four-card trump holding intact. Here are two hands that should play in a 4-3 fit:

<u>Opener</u>	<u>Responder</u>
♠ KJ9	♠ AQ85
♥ 94	♥ T6
♦ KQ532	♦ AJ98
♣ KJ4	♣ Q52

With these two hands, 4♠ is the only game with any chance.

In 3NT, you are off the entire heart suit as well as the ace of clubs; in 5♦, you must lose two hearts and a club. If the defenders play three rounds of hearts, **declarer can trump in the short trump hand** and knock out the ace of clubs, making 4♠ as long as trumps break no worse than 4-2.

When you are playing in a 4-3 fit, **you generally do not want to draw trumps.** The playing strategy is similar to a crossruff — you want to cash all of your side suit winners and then crossruff the hand. Alternatively, you want to ruff some of your losers in dummy, the short trump hand, before drawing trumps. Here are some examples of playing in a 4-3 fit:

```
DLR: North          ♠ 862
VUL: Both           ♥ J82
Matchpoints         ♦ 653
                    ♣ AQ43

  ♠ 43                              ♠ K975
  ♥ Q93                             ♥ T654
  ♦ KQJ2                            ♦ A
  ♣ K875                            ♣ JT92

                    ♠ AQJT
                    ♥ AK7
                    ♦ T9874
                    ♣ 6
```

After two passes, south elected to open 1♠ on his good four-card suit, and north's raise to 2♠ ended the auction. West's lead of the king of diamonds was overtaken by east's ace, and a heart shift was won by declarer's king. Declarer led a club to dummy's queen; when this held, declarer pitched a heart on the ace of clubs, ruffed a club, cashed the ace of hearts, and exited with a diamond. West cashed two diamond tricks and played a third diamond for his partner to ruff. East exited with a heart, ruffed by declarer, who now exited with his last diamond. Declarer scored the last two tricks with the AQ of spades to make his contract.

Here is an example of a good auction that led to a 4-3 fit:

DLR: North   ♠ QT8
VUL: N-S   ♥ AKQJ4
Swiss Teams   ♦ KQ954
      ♣ ——

♠ 7432   ♠ 95
♥ 975   ♥ T632
♦ J82   ♦ A6
♣ KQ3   ♣ AJ752

     ♠ AKJ6
     ♥ 8
     ♦ T73
     ♣ T9864

North	East	South	West
1 ♥	Pass	1 ♠	Pass
3 ♦	Pass	3NT	Pass
4 ♠	Pass	Pass	Pass

Declarer ruffed the opening king of clubs lead, drew trumps, and claimed ten tricks when the hearts divided 4-3.

KEY POINTS

1. In order to be a winning bridge player, you must learn to count out both the high card points and the distribution of the unseen hands.

2. You should always try to combine your chances to make the contract, rather than relying on a finesse without testing your other chances first.

3. Try to cultivate a deceptive style, in order to conceal your assets from your opponents. For example, if dummy has AQxx and you have Kxx, lead low towards the queen. By playing the queen, your RHO may place his partner with the king and won't know where your high card points are located.

4. You should always play the card that you are known, or will be known, to hold. For example, if you hold KJx and declarer successfully finesses the queen, you must drop your king on the second round. Otherwise, the declarer will know that you still hold the king.

5. The Theory of Restricted Choice says that when one of your opponents plays an honor card, the odds are 2 to 1 that the honor is a singleton. Accordingly, you should play the other opponent to have any missing honors in that suit.

6. In order to avoid an enemy trump promotion, it is frequently good strategy to throw a loser on a loser rather than weaken your trump holding.

7. When you are playing in a 4-3 fit, you generally do not want to draw trumps. The playing strategy is similar to a crossruff – you want to cash all of your side suit winners and then crossruff the hand. Alternatively, if your trumps are solid, you want to ruff some of your losers in dummy, the short trump hand, before drawing trumps.

DECLARER PLAY QUIZ

1. Both Vulnerable   <u>Dummy</u>
                              ♠ KQ2
Opening Lead: ♥ QT54
Ten of Spades   ♦ A73
                              ♣ J87

Plan the play
in 6NT   <u>You</u>
                              ♠ AJ7
                              ♥ AK3
                              ♦ KQ54
                              ♣ KQ9

2. Vulnerable versus	<u>Dummy</u>	RHO	You	LHO	Partner
non-vulnerable	♠ 4	1♠	Pass	Pass	2♦
	♥ 54	Pass	3NT	AllPass	
Opening Lead:	♦ AKQ762				
Ten of Hearts	♣ 8743				
East plays the Jack.					

Plan the play
in 3NT   <u>You</u>
                              ♠ AQ8532
                              ♥ A76
                              ♦ 9
                              ♣ AK2

3. Non-vulnerable
versus Vul.

Opening Lead:
Ten of Clubs
East wins the
Ace and returns
the suit.

Plan the play
in 4♥

<u>Dummy</u>
♠ KT43
♥ J83
♦ AQ4
♣ J62

<u>You</u>
♠ QJ
♥ QT9752
♦ K6
♣ KQ7

4. None Vulnerable

Opening Lead:
King of Clubs

Plan the play
in 6♠

<u>Dummy</u>
♠ KQ92
♥ AKT
♦ K952
♣ A6

<u>You</u>
♠ AT875
♥ 953
♦ AQ7
♣ 82

5. Both Vulnerable

Opening Lead:
Eight of Clubs

East wins the nine
and plays the Ace
and King of Clubs.

Plan the play
in 4♥

Dummy
♠ 653
♥ Q754
♦ K76
♣ Q74

You
♠ AKJ
♥ AK632
♦ A84
♣ 63

6. None Vulnerable

Opening Lead:
Four of Diamonds

Plan the play
in 2♥

Dummy
♠ 62
♥ K52
♦ AQJ
♣ KJ865

You
♠ AK83
♥ QT94
♦ 95
♣ 972

ANSWERS

1. **Knock out the ace of clubs** and try to get a count on the other suits before playing hearts. You should play spades and diamonds first in order to get a partial count of the hand. You will discover that your LHO started out with five spades, two clubs and two diamonds, leaving him with four hearts. Cash the ace and king of hearts and take the marked finesse of the ten to make your slam.

2. **Win the first heart trick with the ace** and duck one round of clubs. You must hope for a blocked heart suit to make this hand – in this case, your RHO was dealt KQJ, and your LHO cannot cash his winning hearts. Ducking one round of clubs gives you the additional chance of finding clubs dividing 3-3, as well as the chance of a 3-3 diamond break.

3. **You have no legitimate chance of making this hand** – you are off the ace of clubs, the ace of spades, and the ace and king of trumps. However, you may try for a deceptive play to steal a trick. After you win trick two with the king of clubs, lead the jack of spades from your hand. If LHO has the ace, he may duck this trick. If the jack of spades holds the trick, you can play three rounds of diamonds, pitching your spade loser, and make an impossible contract.

4. **You must pitch your club loser on a good diamond.** Win the ace of clubs and draw trumps, which break 3-1, with your LHO having three. Now play the ace and queen of diamonds from your hand. On the second round of diamonds, RHO follows with the jack. Using the principle of Restricted Choice, you should finesse the nine of diamonds on the third round – when this holds, your

club loser gets discarded on dummy's winning king of diamonds, and you concede a heart trick to make your slam. The full hand may be:

```
                    ♠ KQ92
                    ♥ AKT
                    ♦ K952
                    ♣ A6
   ♠ J43                          ♠ 6
   ♥ 86                           ♥ QJ742
   ♦ T643                         ♦ J8
   ♣ KQ75                         ♣ JT943
                    ♠ AT875
                    ♥ 953
                    ♦ AQ7
                    ♣ 82
```

5. When the opponents continue with a third round of clubs, **pitch your diamond loser instead of trumping**. You will be able to draw trumps on a normal 3-1 trump break, and you will need to take a spade finesse in order to make the contract. The full hand may be as follows:

♠ 653
♥ Q754
♦ K76
♣ Q74

♠ 742   ♠ QT98
♥ JT9   ♥ 8
♦ JT932   ♦ Q5
♣ 82   ♣ AKJT95

♠ AKJ
♥ AK632
♦ A84
♣ 63

Note that if you ruff the third round of clubs with a low trump, west will overruff, and you will eventually lose a diamond trick. If you ruff with a high trump, west simply pitches a side suit card and must come to a trump trick. By making a **loser on loser** play, you avoid the enemy trump promotion.

6. **Take the diamond finesse.** If it wins, cross to your hand with a spade and repeat the finesse. Cash the third diamond, cross to your hand with a high spade, and ruff a spade in dummy. You must come to at least eight tricks as long as you don't play trumps.

CHAPTER 7

DEFENSE

A. <u>Passive Versus Active Defense</u>

There are two approaches to defending a bridge hand: passive and active. In **passive defense**, the goal is not to give anything away and make the declarer go after his own tricks. Safety is the paramount concern. Sequence leads and trump leads, which are safe and don't give away a trick, are preferred leads. If declarer leads a suit and you win a trick in that suit, you lead the same suit back in order to avoid breaking a new suit. In **passive defense**, risky leads away from a high honor are avoided. You hope that declarer will not have enough tricks to make his contract, **provided that the defense does not give away any tricks.**

In **active defense**, you must aggressively go after your tricks even if this involves making risky leads. You go out looking for tricks in a hurry. You lead away from kings and queens; you lead or even underlead aces; you get busy. In **active defense**, you take the chance of giving declarer tricks that he could not make without your help, in the hope of establishing enough tricks for the defense before the declarer has time to make his contract.

How do you decide whether to employ an active or a passive defense? There are two determining factors: 1) The opponents' bidding, and 2) The cards that you hold.

Let us look at the bidding first. Most bidding sequences will give you a general idea of the opponents' combined strength. You should try to determine whether your opponents are stretching for a game or if they have values to spare for their bids. If the opponents have extra values and, given time, they will have a lot of tricks to take, you must get active if you want to have a chance at beating the contract. If, on the other hand, the opponents have stretched to the limit to bid a game, they are likely to fail in their contract provided that you defend **passively** and avoid giving away a trick with an aggressive opening lead.

The second factor is the hand you are dealt. Based on the bidding, you can determine if your cards are lying favorably or unfavorably for the declarer, and whether the suits are breaking well or not. If your cards are lying well for the declarer and his key suits are breaking well for him, you must employ **active defense** and try to establish and take tricks before declarer can throw away his losers on a good side suit. On the other hand, if the cards are lying poorly for the declarer and his suits are not breaking well, the contract is likely to fail if you employ **passive defense** and don't give anything away.

The time that an active defense is called for is **when either the dummy or the declarer can establish a long suit** to pitch away his losers. In this case, the defenders must try to take all the tricks that they can before they go away on the long suit. On the other hand, a passive defense is called for when the declarer cannot set up a long suit for discards. In this case, the defenders can play passively and wait for the tricks that they are entitled to take, and let declarer do all of the guesswork in going after his tricks.

Many bridge hands call for passive defense, making the declarer do his own work. One of the most common defensive errors is to get active when the declarer does not have a ready source of tricks. Many players are reluctant to sit back and defend passively – they attack suits, giving away tricks and enabling the declarer to make extra tricks that he could not achieve on his own initiative. If you can resist the temptation to get active when passive defense is called for, your results will improve dramatically.

Here are some examples of active versus passive defense on opening lead:

You	RHO	LHO
♠ T98	1♦	1♥
♥ K54	1NT	Pass
♦ AJ94		
♣ Q76		

Neither of your opponents has shown a long suit in the bidding, and you have diamonds well stopped. Make the passive lead of the **ten of spades** and make declarer go after his own tricks.

You	LHO	RHO
♠ T76	1♣	1♠
♥ KJ4	3♣	3♠
♦ JT97	4♠	Pass
♣ J83		

Dummy will show up with a long, strong club suit, and you know that both clubs and spades are breaking well for the declarer. You must get active and go after your tricks right away – if you make a passive lead such as a trump or the jack of diamonds, declarer will draw trumps and pitch his losers away on dummy's good clubs. Therefore, you should lead the **four of hearts** in order to take the tricks that your side is entitled to, before they go away. If it turns out that your heart lead cost a trick, it didn't really matter - declarer would have thrown away his heart losers on dummy's good clubs anyway.

Here is an example of **active defense** in the context of a complete hand:

DLR: East   ♠ J93
VUL: Both   ♥ QT4
Rubber Bridge   ♦ KQJ94
              ♣ JT

♠ T54		♠ AKQ76
♥ 85		♥ A2
♦ 8765		♦ T3
♣ Q952		♣ K864

              ♠ 82
              ♥ KJ9763
              ♦ A2
              ♣ A73

South	West	North	East
			1 ♠
2 ♥	Pass	4 ♥	All Pass

West leads the four of spades, and after cashing two spade tricks, east knows that declarer has no more spades. If east continues with a third round of spades, declarer ruffs, knocks out the ace of trump, and pitches his club losers away on dummy's good diamonds. In order to defeat the contract, east must **shift to a club** at trick three in order to set up a club trick for the defense. Looking at a long, strong suit in dummy, east must employ an **active defense**, since any club losers declarer might have will go away on the diamonds in dummy.

Here is an example of **passive defense:**

DLR: South
VUL: None
Matchpoints

♠ A62
♥ K85
♦ AQJ2
♣ K86

♠ J953
♥ QT63
♦ T98
♣ T2

♠ 87
♥ 9742
♦ 753
♣ QJ97

♠ KQT4
♥ AJ
♦ K64
♣ A543

South	West	North	East
1NT	Pass	4NT	Pass
6NT	Pass	Pass	Pass

West made the passive lead of the **ten of diamonds** against the opponents' slam. With spades not breaking and the heart finesse offside, declarer only had eleven tricks. Note that making an attacking lead of either major suit presents declarer with his twelfth trick.

B. Obvious Shift Carding *

When you are defending a hand and partner leads a suit at trick one, the primary signal that you provide is **attitude** – you play a high card if you want partner to continue that suit, and you

---

* This portion of the book is based on the Granovetters' excellent book on this topic, *A Switch in Time.*

play a low card if you would like partner to shift to another suit. Notice that **playing a low card does not tell partner what suit to shift to** – it just indicates that you would like partner to shift to another suit. Partner should look at dummy and should generally shift to dummy's weaker side suit. Dummy's weak side suit is called the **Obvious Shift**.

In simple attitude situations, you give attitude pertaining **only to the suit that partner has led.** For example, if partner leads an ace (ace from ace-king) against a suit and you hold Q93, you play the nine in order to encourage partner to continue the suit; if you hold 843, you play the three to tell your partner that you have no help for him in that suit. Either you like the suit or you don't like the suit, and you signal accordingly.

However, what if you want your partner to shift to another suit? Let us extend the position to cover two suits in dummy:

	Dummy		
Ace of ♠ led	♠ T65		
	♥ K93	HAND 1	HAND 2
		♠ Q74	♠ T74
		♥ AQJ	♥ 872

On Hand 1, you should play the four of spades in order to get partner to shift to hearts, **even though you have help for partner in spades.** On Hand 2, you may be best off signalling with the seven of spades, even though you have no help for your partner in the spade suit, **in order to prevent partner from making a disastrous heart shift!**

As you can see from this example, simple attitude signals are not very effective. How often has your partner sent you a discouraging signal and you had no idea of what suit to play next? The solution to this defensive problem is to combine standard attitude signals with the **Obvious Shift Principle.** Simply stated, in most situations, a discouraging signal when partner leads an honor card and will hold the trick conveys two messages: 1) You do not like partner's suit, and 2) You can stand a shift to the **Obvious Shift** suit, which is generally dummy's weakest suit. Note that if you cannot stand a shift to dummy's weak suit, **you would tend to give false encouragement to partner's opening lead.**

The **Obvious Shift Principle** is not a difficult concept, but it requires both defenders to think. The **Obvious Shift Principle** is based on attitude signals, but **it extends the attitude signal to the entire hand** rather than just simply to the suit that your partner has led.

On opening lead, when third hand has a choice of cards to play, he can tell his partner whether or not he likes the suit led. However, if you are looking just at the suit led and you send a signal based only on your holding in that suit (simple attitude), you are not giving your partner enough information. You must ask yourself: "Does continuing this suit help us?" and "Do I want partner to shift to another suit?" The answer to the second question might be "yes" even if you have strength in the suit that your partner has led! Playing the **Obvious Shift Principle** conveys a great deal of information to your partner at trick one. You can immediately indicate to your partner whether or not you would like him to switch to the weak side suit in the dummy (the **obvious shift**). The **Obvious Shift Principle** applies even when there is a singleton in dummy – a high card says continue the suit and make dummy ruff, a low card says make the Obvious Shift.

Many players mistakenly think that suit preference applies when partner plays a low card at trick one. This is not correct thinking. Partner's play at trick one is an attitude situation – a low card says you are not interested in the suit that partner has led, but it does not indicate which suit partner should shift to. Partner must look at the dummy and shift to dummy's weak side suit.

The following example is from the Granovetters' book, *A Shift In Time*:

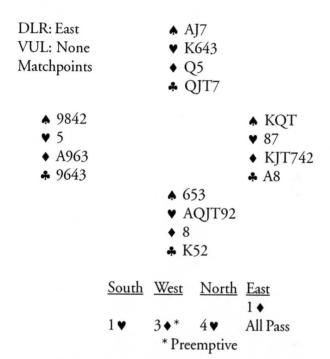

DLR: East
VUL: None
Matchpoints

♠ AJ7
♥ K643
♦ Q5
♣ QJT7

♠ 9842
♥ 5
♦ A963
♣ 9643

♠ KQT
♥ 87
♦ KJT742
♣ A8

♠ 653
♥ AQJT92
♦ 8
♣ K52

South	West	North	East
			1 ♦
1 ♥	3 ♦ *	4 ♥	All Pass

* Preemptive

West leads the ace of diamonds, and east needs his partner to shift to spades in order to defeat the contract, so he plays the two of diamonds, asking for a shift. West must now use his judgement in deciding which suit to shift to. Since dummy has a solid club sequence, there is no future in shifting to clubs, as a club shift will only set up club winners in the dummy. West therefore shifts to a spade at trick two, setting up two spade tricks for the defenders before declarer can establish the club suit to discard his spade losers. Note that the Obvious Shift is never a suit with three touching honors, and that only a spade shift at trick two defeats the contract.

Here is the other side of the coin:

DLR: West   ♠ KQ5
VUL: Both   ♥ K53
Matchpoints   ♦ J964
              ♣ T64

♠ A76   ♠ J842
♥ AT97   ♥ J84
♦ KQT7   ♦ 832
♣ 72   ♣ A53

              ♠ T93
              ♥ Q62
              ♦ A5
              ♣ KQJ98

South	West	North	East
	1 ♦	Pass	1 ♠
2 ♣	Pass	3 ♣	All Pass

West leads the ace of spades because of partner's 1♠ response, and **east should play the eight of spades, asking for a spade continuation.** Obviously, east cannot like spades when dummy has the high king and queen, but the message east is conveying to his partner is **not to shift to another suit.** Since east cannot stand a shift to either red suit, he does best to encourage spades. This will result in the defenders taking five tricks – one spade, two hearts, one diamond and one club – to defeat the contract. Note that if west shifts to either red suit at trick two, he gives away a trick and declarer makes the contract.

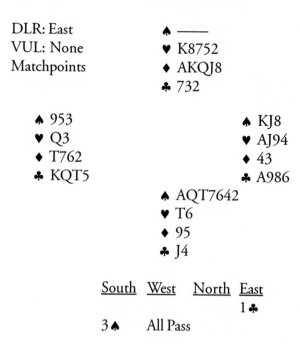

DLR: East
VUL: None
Matchpoints

```
                    ♠ ——
                    ♥ K8752
                    ♦ AKQJ8
                    ♣ 732

    ♠ 953                           ♠ KJ8
    ♥ Q3                            ♥ AJ94
    ♦ T762                          ♦ 43
    ♣ KQT5                          ♣ A986

                    ♠ AQT7642
                    ♥ T6
                    ♦ 95
                    ♣ J4
```

South	West	North	East
			1♣
3♠	All Pass		

On the king of clubs lead, east played the six, his lowest club, asking for the obvious shift. West shifted to the queen of hearts at trick two, and the contract had to go down two – declarer had to lose two clubs, two hearts and two trump tricks. Note that if west does not shift to a heart at trick two, he never gets another chance to lead a heart through, and declarer can hold the contract to down one due to the 3-3 trump break.

```
DLR: West            ♠ QT52
VUL: Both            ♥ 42
Matchpoints          ♦ AKQ87
                     ♣ Q3

    ♠ A4                          ♠ 7
    ♥ KJ976                       ♥ T853
    ♦ 4                           ♦ J932
    ♣ KT542                       ♣ A987

                     ♠ KJ9863
                     ♥ AQ
                     ♦ T65
                     ♣ J6
```

South	West	North	East
	1♥	2♦	3♥*
3♠	Pass	4♠	All Pass
	* Preemptive		

West led his singleton diamond, and east encouraged with the nine, **denying any interest in the obvious shift suit, hearts.** When west got in with the ace of trumps, he had no alternative except to play a club. This resulted in down one when partner won the ace of clubs and gave west his diamond ruff. Notice that if east plays a low diamond at trick one, west would probably shift to a heart after winning the ace of trumps in an attempt to put his partner in for a diamond ruff. This defense would enable declarer to make an overtrick!

Here is another example of how obvious shift applies even when dummy has a singleton:

DLR: South
VUL: E-W
Swiss Teams

```
                     ♠ K54
                     ♥ KJT973
                     ♦ 6
                     ♣ J76

    ♠ 9762                           ♠ A83
    ♥ 4                              ♥ 8652
    ♦ AKT4                           ♦ Q982
    ♣ A954                           ♣ 82

                     ♠ QJT
                     ♥ AQ
                     ♦ J753
                     ♣ KQT3
```

South	West	North	East
1NT	Pass	4♦	Pass
4♥	Pass	Pass	Pass

When west leads the ace of diamonds, east encourages with the nine. With length in the trump suit, east wants to force the dummy to ruff so that east's small trumps will eventually become winners. Continued diamond leads result in tapping out the dummy. Declarer will lose control of the hand and go down one.

C. Suit Preference Defense

One area of bridge in which the expert defender maximizes the number of tricks that his side takes is the use of spot cards to indicate suit preference to his partner. There are many opportunities to use the size of your spot card to indicate suit preference. Here is an example:

DLR: South   ♠ KJ7
VUL: E-W   ♥ 65
Matchpoints   ♦ AQT87
     ♣ J43

```
        ♠ KJ7
        ♥ 65
        ♦ AQT87
        ♣ J43

♠ A65              ♠ T942
♥ QT872            ♥ KJ3
♦ 64               ♦ K52
♣ 762              ♣ T95

        ♠ Q83
        ♥ A94
        ♦ J93
        ♣ AKQ8
```

South	West	North	East
1NT	Pass	3NT	All Pass

West leads the seven of hearts against south's 3NT contract, and declarer holds up his ace until the third round. Since all of his spot cards are equals, west can indicate suit preference to his partner by the size of the spot card he plays on the third round. West indicates a spade entry to his partner by **playing the queen of hearts on the third round**, showing suit preference for the high ranking suit. Without this signal, east would probably return a club into dummy's weakness when he wins the king of diamonds.

Another situation where suit preference signals apply is when partner leads a suit in which dummy has a singleton. Since you couldn't possibly want the suit continued (dummy will trump the second round), the size of your spot card shows suit preference between the two remaining suits*. Here is a spectacular example of this type of suit preference signalling:

DLR: East	♠ 4		
VUL: Both	♥ KJ53		
Swiss Teams	♦ A3		
	♣ QJT982		

♠ K932		♠ AJT765
♥ 9		♥ 42
♦ T8754		♦ KJ6
♣ 654		♣ A3

♠ Q8
♥ AQT876
♦ Q92
♣ K7

South	West	North	East
			1♠
2♥	3♠*	4♥	4♠
Pass	Pass	5♣	Pass
5♥	All Pass		
	* Preemptive		

* This does not apply if you are playing Obvious Shift defense. Playing Obvious Shift, a low card would ask for the obvious shift suit, and a high card would ask for a continuation of the suit that was led, even when dummy has a singleton.

West didn't rate to be on lead too often with this hand. Ideally, west wanted to lay down an ace to look at dummy; since he didn't see any aces in his hand, he improvised by leading the king of spades. Partner followed suit to this trick with the jack of spades, **asking for a shift to the higher ranking side suit, diamonds.** West duly shifted to a diamond at trick two, and the contract had to go down one. Note that this is the only defense that defeats the contract.

Here is another example of this type of suit preference:

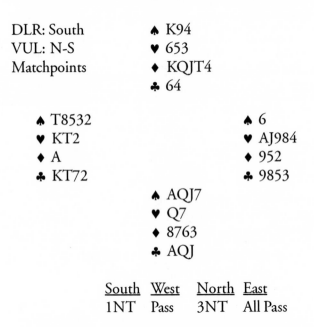

DLR: South	♠ K94
VUL: N-S	♥ 653
Matchpoints	♦ KQJT4
	♣ 64

♠ T8532	♠ 6
♥ KT2	♥ AJ984
♦ A	♦ 952
♣ KT72	♣ 9853

| ♠ AQJ7 |
| ♥ Q7 |
| ♦ 8763 |
| ♣ AQJ |

South	West	North	East
1NT	Pass	3NT	All Pass

West led the three of spades to partner's six and declarer's jack. When declarer leads a diamond at trick two and west wins the ace, east can signal suit preference by the size of the spot card he plays in diamonds. Since there is no future in spades, the choice is between hearts and diamonds. When east follows with the nine of diamonds, west shifts to a heart, and the defenders take six tricks. There is no point in giving count in diamonds, since the suit is already running.

When you lead the ace from ace-king and your partner follows with the queen, showing the jack, you have the option of underleading your king to your partner's jack. If you exercise this option, the size of the spot card you lead to your partner should be a suit preference signal for what suit to return. The following hand illustrates this point:

DLR: South   ♠ JT6
VUL: N-S   ♥ 97
Matchpoints   ♦ QJT8
       ♣ QJT8

♠ A4   ♠ 52
♥ AKT642   ♥ QJ3
♦ 97   ♦ 6432
♣ K42   ♣ 9763

      ♠ KQ9873
      ♥ 85
      ♦ AK5
      ♣ A5

South	West	North	East
1♠	2♥	2♠	Pass
4♠	All Pass		

West leads the ace of hearts and east plays the queen, showing the jack. West now continues with the two of hearts, **showing suit preference for clubs**, the lowest ranking suit. East shifts to a club at trick three, and the contract has to go down one.

Notice that without the suit preference signal, east would not know which minor suit to shift to. If east does not shift to clubs, declarer knocks out the ace of trumps, draws trump, and pitches his club loser on dummy's fourth diamond.

When partner leads an obvious singleton against a suit contract and you cannot win the trick, **the size of your spot card
should be a suit preference signal, indicating your entry to give
partner his ruff.** Here are some examples of this principle in the
context of a complete hand:

DLR: North   ♠ KJT5
VUL: E-W   ♥ J7
Matchpoints   ♦ AQ8
                 ♣ K543

♠ A   ♠ 97432
♥ 642   ♥ A9
♦ T93   ♦ KJ74
♣ AQJ872   ♣ T9

             ♠ Q86
             ♥ KQT853
             ♦ 652
             ♣ 6

North-South got to 2♥, declared by south. West led his singleton ace of spades and east followed with the nine, his highest spade,
requesting a shift to the higher ranking side suit, diamonds. The
ten of diamonds was covered by dummy's queen and east's king,
and east continued with the seven of spades, **as a repeat suit preference for diamonds.** West ruffed with the four of hearts and continued with a diamond to dummy's ace. Declarer led the jack of
hearts, but east rose with the ace as west echoed with the two of
hearts to show a third trump*. The defenders collected another
spade ruff, the ace of clubs and another diamond trick for down
two.

* A **trump echo** is a high-low signal in trumps, which is generally used to show three trumps. This is the opposite of standard
suit signals, where a high-low signal would show an even number
of cards.

Here is another example:

DLR: East   ♠ 74
VUL: Both   ♥ T83
Matchpoints   ♦ QT7
       ♣ KQT87

```
        ♠ K82              ♠ 65
        ♥ AJ94             ♥ KQ72
        ♦ K6532            ♦ A84
        ♣ 4                ♣ 6532
              ♠ AQJT93
              ♥ 65
              ♦ J9
              ♣ AJ9
```

East passed, and south opened 1♠ and rebid 2♠ over his partner's 1NT response. West led his singleton four of clubs, declarer played dummy's king, and east played the six of clubs, his highest club, **as a suit preference signal for hearts**. Declarer now took a losing trump finesse, and the roof caved in. West underled his ace of hearts to partner's queen, received a club ruff, and led a heart to his partner's king. East now made the good play of cashing the ace of diamonds in case his partner was out of trumps, but west followed with the two of diamonds, expressing no interest in diamonds. East now gave his partner a second club ruff, and west cashed the king of diamonds for the seventh defensive trick.

Of course, the declarer could have done better by playing a spade to the ace followed by the queen of spades, but at matchpoints the lure of the finesse was too difficult for the declarer to resist.

D. <u>When To Lead Trumps</u>

There are three occasions when a trump lead is mandatory: 1) Partner passes your takeout double at the one- or two-level; 2) The opponents are sacrificing against your game, and your side has most of the high card strength; 3) Declarer has shown a two-suited hand, dummy takes a preference to declarer's second suit, and you have strength in declarer's first bid suit. Let us look at examples of each of these situations:

1. <u>Partner Passes Your Takeout Double At A Low Level</u>

To justify the pass, partner must have a very strong trump holding, and leading trumps has the effect of drawing declarer's trumps. Here is an example:

DLR: South	♠ 62	
VUL: Both	♥ 6542	
Matchpoints	♦ 7	
	♣ K87652	

♠ T		♠ AQJ98
♥ AQ97		♥ JT
♦ KQJ4		♦ 9853
♣ QJ93		♣ T4

	♠ K7543	
	♥ K83	
	♦ AT62	
	♣ A	

South opens 1♠, west makes a takeout double, and east converts it into a penalty double by passing. If west leads the king of diamonds, declarer wins the ace, cashes the ace of clubs, and ruffs a diamond in dummy. Declarer cashes dummy's king of clubs, pitching a heart loser, and plays another club from dummy. If east ruffs, declarer overruffs and ruffs another diamond with dummy's last trump. Declarer has six tricks, and escapes for down one. **Look at the difference if west leads his singleton ten of trumps.** East overtakes with the ace, and continues with the queen of spades to declarer's king. Declarer can never get to the dummy, and only takes three tricks – one spade, one diamond, and one club – and E-W collect a profitable penalty of +1100. One of the times that a trump lead is mandatory is when partner passes your takeout double, converting it into penalties. Partner is not passing out of weakness – partner has values, and must have a very strong holding in the opponent's trump suit to want to double the opponents at a low level.

2. <u>The Opponents Are Sacrificing</u>

The opponents frequently have some distribution when they sacrifice at a high level, so a trump lead is usually effective. The only way the opponents can take tricks when your side has most of the points is to crossruff the hand, scoring their trumps separately, and a trump lead is the best defense against a crossruff. Here is an example:

DLR: East   ♠ AJT
VUL: None   ♥ J654
Matchpoints   ♦ 4
                          ♣ QJT74

♠ 8654   ♠ ——
♥ Q2   ♥ AKT73
♦ AQ983   ♦ J62
♣ A2   ♣ K9653

                          ♠ KQ9732
                          ♥ 98
                          ♦ KT75
                          ♣ 8

East opened 1♥, south made a weak jump overcall of 2♠, west
bid 3♦, and north jumped to 4♠. After two passes, west doubled,
which ended the auction.

Realizing that his side held most of the points, west led a
trump, and continued leading trumps every time he obtained the
lead. This prevented declarer from ruffing two diamonds in the
dummy, and declarer had to lose six tricks for –500, adequate
compensation for east-west's non-vulnerable game.

3. Declarer Has Bid Two Suits, And You Have Strength In Declarer's First Bid Suit

When dummy takes a preference to declarer's second suit by passing, dummy will be very short in declarer's first bid suit. If you have strength in declarer's first bid suit, the way to protect your tricks in this suit is **by leading trumps.** Here is an example:

DLR: South	♠ 4
VUL: Both	♥ 9752
Matchpoints	♦ QJ4
	♣ QJ763

♠ QT87	♠ K65
♥ QJT	♥ A863
♦ 7653	♦ A8
♣ K4	♣ T982

♠ AJ932
♥ K4
♦ KT92
♣ A5

South opens 1♠, north responds 1NT, and south rebids 2♦, which ends the auction. With strength in declarer's first bid suit, west should lead a trump. On a trump lead and continuation, declarer can only trump one spade in dummy, and must lose two spade tricks. On the queen of hearts lead and a heart continuation, declarer can trump two spades in dummy and make his contract.

When the opponents find a fit by means of some distributional gadget such as Michaels or Flannery, **a trump lead is often the best defense.** Against a grand slam, your objective is generally to make the safest lead possible, which is generally a trump lead.

When Not to Lead Trumps

Although there are many situations when the opening leader should automatically lead trumps, there are numerous occasions when far too many players lead trumps when an **active defense** is called for. Here is a typical example:

```
DLR: South              ♠ KT84
VUL: Both               ♥ 82
Swiss Teams             ♦ KQJ84
                        ♣ 76

  ♠ 65                           ♠ 72
  ♥ KJ74                         ♥ QT53
  ♦ A63                          ♦ 975
  ♣ KJ95                         ♣ A842

                        ♠ AQJ93
                        ♥ A96
                        ♦ T2
                        ♣ QT3
```

South opens 1♠, west makes a takeout double, and north jumps to 4♠, which ends the auction. On opening lead, west feels that it is dangerous to lead away from any of his tenaces, so he makes the "safe" lead of a trump. This results in declarer drawing trumps, knocking out the ace of diamonds, and making ten tricks.

As you can see, a trump lead on this type of hand is by no means a safe lead. A trump lead gives the defense no chance whatsoever to defeat the contract. The situation when dummy has raised an opening bid of one of a major to game is usually a dangerous one. Occasionally, dummy will have a strong side suit that can easily be established to provide discards for declarer's losers.

Looking at the west hand in the example above, it should be clear that if dummy has a side suit that can be established, that suit must be diamonds. Therefore, an attacking lead in either hearts or clubs must be made **before the diamond suit becomes estab-**

lished. This results in defeating the contract, as the defenders establish three tricks in clubs and hearts before the ace of diamonds is knocked out.

The basic principle is that when dummy may show up with a long suit that can become established, an **active defense** is called for. The defenders must go after their tricks quickly before dummy's side suit can be established. Leading trumps is **passive defense**, which is appropriate only when there is no long, strong suit in either the declarer's hand or in dummy.

E. Maintain Parity

Whenever you are defending and you see a four-card suit in the dummy, or declarer has revealed a four-card suit in the bidding, and you also hold four cards in this suit, **you must hold on to all four cards in this suit** at all cost. You are the only one who can protect this suit, and if you throw one card away, the fourth card will become a winner. Here are some examples of maintaining parity:

```
DLR: South        ♠ 853
VUL: None         ♥ AJ73
Matchpoints       ♦ QJ65
                  ♣ 87

  ♠ KQJ97                        ♠ 62
  ♥ Q6                           ♥ T942
  ♦ T97                          ♦ 842
  ♣ A65                          ♣ JT92
                  ♠ AT4
                  ♥ K85
                  ♦ AK3
                  ♣ KQ43
```

South	West	North	East
1♣	1♠	DBL	Pass
3NT	All Pass		

Declarer wins the second spade trick and runs four rounds of diamonds. On the fourth round, **east must pitch a club and hold on to all four of his hearts.** If east throws a heart away, dummy's fourth heart will become high for declarer's ninth trick.

DLR: South   ♠ J3
VUL: N-S   ♥ Q73
Rubber Bridge   ♦ 643
                  ♣ AJ432

♠ T65   ♠ 982
♥ JT96   ♥ AK4
♦ J8   ♦ T752
♣ 9865   ♣ KQT

                  ♠ AKQ74
                  ♥ 852
                  ♦ AKQ9
                  ♣ 7

South	West	North	East
1♠	Pass	1NT	Pass
3♦	Pass	3♠	Pass
4♠	All Pass		

The defenders take the first three heart tricks, and east shifts to the king of clubs at trick four. Declarer wins dummy's ace and runs five rounds of trumps, forcing east to make two discards. In order to defeat the hand, **east must throw away his club winner and hold on to all four of his diamonds.** Since east knows that the declarer has four diamonds from the bidding, he must maintain parity. Of course, east should be able to count out declarer's hand from the bidding and the play so far, and realize that declarer must have a singleton club.

F. <u>Tricks in the Trump Suit</u>

There are three ways the defenders can promote trump tricks for themselves: 1) Forcing the declarer to ruff until he loses control of the hand; 2) Trump promotion; and 3) Uppercut. Let us look at each of these three techniques.

1. <u>Defending With Trump Length</u>

Whenever you are defending with trump length, **you frequently want to lead your side's long suit.** Your objective is to force the declarer to ruff in the long trump hand, causing him to lose control of the hand. For example, if you start with four trumps and the declarer has five trumps, forcing him to ruff brings him down to your trump length. If you force declarer to ruff again, he will have fewer trumps than you and will lose control of the hand. This technique is known as the **forcing game.**

If you hold the high trump as well as length in the trump suit, you must be careful as to when you win your high trump. If declarer and dummy are both void in the suit that you are forcing declarer with, you must wait to win your high trump **until dummy, the short trump hand, is exhausted of trumps.** Once dummy has no trumps left, you can continue to force the declarer in your long suit.

You generally do not want to lead a singleton when you have trump length. Even if you obtain a ruff, you are shortening your trumps, making it easy for declarer to draw your trumps when he regains the lead.

Here are some examples of defending with trump length:

DLR: North   ♠ 642
VUL: N-S   ♥ QT
Matchpoints   ♦ J753
                    ♣ AKQJ

♠ A875   ♠ 3
♥ 4   ♥ A76532
♦ AQ984   ♦ KT62
♣ 432   ♣ 85

                    ♠ KQJT9
                    ♥ KJ98
                    ♦ ——
                    ♣ T976

North	East	South	West
1♣	Pass	1♠	Pass
1NT	Pass	3♥	Pass
3♠	Pass	4♠	All Pass

It is so important to lead your long suit when you have length in trumps that you should be willing to lead the ace from a suit headed by the AQ. West therefore led the ace of diamonds, and declarer ruffed the opening diamond lead, **reducing his trump length to west's level.** Declarer now played trumps, and west won his ace on the third round, exhausting dummy of trumps. Another diamond lead forced declarer to ruff with his last trump. As soon as the defenders obtained the lead, they were able to cash three diamond tricks, to go along with the ace of hearts and two trump tricks, for down three.

Notice what happens on this hand if west leads his singleton heart. The defenders get the ace of hearts, a ruff, and the ace of trumps, and declarer makes his contract. The worst thing you can do when you have length in trumps is to lead a short suit, trying for a ruff. Declarer will be delighted to let you trump in the long trump hand - this will make it easy for declarer to set up his long suit, draw trumps and claim.

DLR: South   ♠ JT8
VUL: E-W   ♥ 875
Matchpoints   ♦ AKT
             ♣ QJ98

West		East
♠ A652		♠ 7
♥ KQ932		♥ AJT
♦ J4		♦ 97632
♣ 72		♣ T654

              ♠ KQ943
              ♥ 64
              ♦ Q85
              ♣ AK3

South	West	North	East
1 ♠	Pass	1NT*	Pass
2 ♣	Pass	3 ♠	Pass
4 ♠	All Pass		

* Forcing

With length in trumps, west led the king of hearts from his long suit. Three rounds of hearts reduced south to four trumps. When south played trumps, **west waited until the third round to win his ace**, exhausting dummy of trumps. A fourth heart forced declarer to ruff with his last trump, and the defenders subsequently took another trump trick and the fifth heart for down two. Of course, declarer could have played for down one by switching to a minor suit after two rounds of trumps, but most declarers will go down the extra trick in an attempt to make the contract.

```
DLR: South          ♠ 643
VUL: N-S            ♥ QJ5
Rubber Bridge       ♦ 7632
                    ♣ AJ8

♠ T952                              ♠ 7
♥ 4                                 ♥ A8632
♦ AK84                              ♦ JT95
♣ 7432                              ♣ T96

                    ♠ AKQJ8
                    ♥ KT97
                    ♦ Q
                    ♣ KQ5
```

South opened 1♠ and became the declarer in 4♠. West led the ace of diamonds and continued with the king of diamonds, forcing declarer to ruff. Declarer drew three rounds of trump, finding out about the 4–1 break. When declarer knocked out the ace of hearts, the defenders continued diamonds, forcing declarer to ruff with his last trump. The defenders were now able to cash a trump trick and the fourth diamond for down one.

Remember the basic principle: **When you are long in trumps, lead your side's long suit.** Your objective is to force the long trump hand to ruff and lose control of the hand.

2. Trump Promotion

When your partner leads a suit that both you and the declarer are void in, frequently you can obtain a trump trick that you could not obtain under your own power. This is known as a **trump promotion.** For example:

	Dummy	
<u>You</u>	T96	<u>Partner</u>
J42		3
	Declarer	
	AKQ875	

If this is the trump position and partner leads a suit that both you and the declarer are void in, you must get a trump trick with your jack. If declarer ruffs high, you will pitch a card in a side suit, and if declarer ruffs low, you can overruff with the jack.

The best way for the declarer to counteract an enemy trump promotion is to make a **Loser on Loser** play (see Chapter 6). However, if declarer has no loser to pitch, the trump promotion will succeed.

Here are some examples of trump promotion:

DLR: North
VUL: None
Matchpoints

♠ AK8
♥ J92
♦ AKQT76
♣ A

♠ T92
♥ AKQ843
♦ 52
♣ T2

♠ Q7
♥ T
♦ J943
♣ J98743

♠ J6543
♥ 765
♦ 8
♣ KQ65

North	East	South	West
1 ♦	Pass	1 ♠	3 ♥
4 ♥	Pass	4 ♠	All Pass

West led his three top hearts against south's 4♠ contract. On the second and third heart, east discarded the three of diamonds and the three of clubs, **showing no interest in clubs or diamonds.** West therefore continued with a fourth round of hearts, and east had to score the queen of trumps for the setting trick.

DLR: North
VUL: N-S
Matchpoints

♠ A652
♥ AJT
♦ A763
♣ 73

♠ KJ87
♥ Q
♦ 54
♣ AKQT54

♠ T94
♥ 9832
♦ QJ98
♣ J8

♠ Q3
♥ K7654
♦ KT2
♣ 962

North	East	South	West
1 ♦	Pass	1 ♥	DBL
2 ♥	Pass	Pass	3 ♣
Pass	Pass	3 ♥	All Pass

West led the ace and king of clubs, and continued with a third high club when his partner echoed in clubs. When dummy trumped this trick with the ten of hearts, it promoted east's nine of hearts into the setting trick when west turned up with the singleton queen of hearts. Declarer lost two clubs, one spade, one diamond and one heart for down one.

DLR: North   ♠ AKQ
VUL: E-W   ♥ K3
Swiss Teams   ♦ AJ52
             ♣ JT63

♠ 4		♠ J73
♥ JT97		♥ AQ85
♦ 9764		♦ T83
♣ 9842		♣ A75

♠ T98652
♥ 642
♦ KQ
♣ KQ

North	East	South	West
1 ♦	Pass	1 ♠	Pass
2NT	Pass	4 ♠	All Pass

West led the jack of hearts, and after taking two heart tricks, east saw that **he could promote a trump trick for himself by making dummy ruff a third heart.** Proper defensive technique is to cash the ace of clubs at trick three just in case declarer held a stiff club and just two hearts. When dummy ruffs the third round of hearts, east must score the setting trick with the jack of spades.

Looking at all four hands, one can observe that N-S can make at least nine tricks in notrump. However, it is certainly a normal action for south to bid 4S over his partner's jump to 2NT.

Here is an example of spectacular defense by the great Howard
Schenken:

DLR: East	♠ T54
VUL: Both	♥ K9
Rubber Bridge	♦ J
	♣ KJ86432

```
♠ 8                                      ♠ AKQ962
♥ JT5                                     ♥ 3
♦ T986542                                 ♦ 73
♣ AQ                                      ♣ T975
                    ♠ J73
                    ♥ AQ87642
                    ♦ AKQ
                    ♣ ———
```

East opened 2♠, and south jumped to 4♥, which ended the
auction. Schenken, sitting west, led his singleton spade, and on
partner's two other high spades, **Schenken pitched the queen and
the ace of clubs.** When partner now led a club, Schenken's trump
holding became promoted into the setting trick.

An important trump promotion principle is that when declarer ruffs a side suit that you are also void in, **do not be in a rush
to overruff the declarer.** You can frequently gain a trump trick by
simply discarding a side suit loser instead of overruffing. Here are
some examples of this principle:

DLR: West   ♠ 652
VUL: N-S   ♥ AQ
Swiss Teams   ♦ KJT96
            ♣ 532

♠ KT4   ♠ 9
♥ J76532   ♥ T8
♦ 742   ♦ 853
♣ K   ♣ AQT9864

♠ AQJ873
♥ K94
♦ AQ
♣ J7

South	West	North	East
	Pass	Pass	3♣
3♠	Pass	4♠	All Pass

West led his singleton king of clubs, and east overtook with the ace, cashed the queen, and continued with the ten of clubs. Declarer ruffed this trick with the jack of spades, and if west overruffs with the king, that is the last trick for the defense. Declarer gets to his hand and plays the ace and queen of trumps, drawing trumps, and claims the rest. However, if west simply pitches a side suit card on the queen of spades, **his trump holding of KT4 becomes promoted into two tricks.** When declarer plays the ace, he follows with the four, and he now takes two trump tricks with the king and ten of spades over declarer's queen.

DLR: East   ♠ 54
VUL: Both   ♥ T973
Rubber Bridge   ♦ KJ53
               ♣ KJ2

♠ Q962   ♠ 3
♥ 86   ♥ AKQJ2
♦ T98   ♦ 764
♣ T765   ♣ Q983

                ♠ AKJT87
                ♥ 54
                ♦ AQ2
                ♣ A4

South	West	North	East
			1♥
DBL	Pass	2♦	Pass
2♠	Pass	3♠	Pass
4♠	All Pass		

West led the eight of hearts, and east cashed two high hearts and led a third high heart, trumped by declarer with the jack. If west overruffs with the queen, that is the last trick for the defense – declarer can draw trumps and claim. However, if west pitches a diamond or a club on the jack of spades, his trump holding becomes promoted into two tricks, and the contract goes down one.

Whenever you have a natural trump trick that cannot go away and declarer ruffs a trick with an honor, **it is almost always right to refuse to overruff.** Frequently, you gain an extra trump trick through promotion, and at worst you break even and get the one trump trick that you were always entitled to.

3. Uppercut

An **uppercut** is a special type of trump promotion in which one defender ruffs with a high trump, promoting a trump trick for his partner. For example:

You	Partner
J4	Q7

If this is your side's holding in trumps, you are not entitled to any trump tricks. Declarer will draw trumps with the ace and the king, and your honors will fall. However, if you lead a suit that your partner and the declarer are void in and your partner trumps with the queen, your trump holding will become promoted into a trick. This play is known as an **uppercut**. Here is an example:

```
DLR: North        ♠ T864
VUL: None         ♥ AK
Matchpoints       ♦ J87
                  ♣ AKQJ


♠ J5                             ♠ Q
♥ T642                           ♥ J983
♦ AKQ5                           ♦ 943
♣ 942                            ♣ T8752

                  ♠ AK9732
                  ♥ Q75
                  ♦ T62
                  ♣ 6
```

North opened 1♣, and south became the declarer in 4♠. After cashing the ace, king and queen of diamonds, west saw no hope for a trick in the side suits. Therefore, he continued with the thirteenth diamond, and when his partner ruffed with the queen, it promoted a trump trick for west for the setting trick.

When you are looking for an uppercut, **do not play a high card in your suit**. If you want to get partner to trump with his highest trump, play a low card to ensure that your partner will trump the trick. Here is an example:

DLR: East	♠ 4	
VUL: N-S	♥ T83	
Matchpoints	♦ KJ9	
	♣ AKQ965	

♠ KT2		♠ 93
♥ AKQ764		♥ 92
♦ 83		♦ 76542
♣ 43		♣ JT87

	♠ AQJ8765	
	♥ J5	
	♦ AQT	
	♣ 2	

South	West	North	East
			Pass
1♠	2♥	3♣	Pass
4♠	All Pass		

West cashed two high hearts and tried for an uppercut **by leading a low heart at trick three**. East duly ruffed with the nine, promoting a second trump trick for west. If west continues with a high heart, most players in the east seat would pitch a card in a side suit rather than ruffing high.

An uppercut can be effective even with a relatively low spot card in the trump suit. In the following hand, the eight of trumps was effective in promoting a trump trick:

DLR: North
VUL: N-S
Rubber Bridge

♠ 963
♥ AK
♦ AKJT5
♣ 954

♠ AT2
♥ 863
♦ 6
♣ AKQ863

♠ 84
♥ T7542
♦ 9872
♣ T2

♠ KQJ75
♥ QJ9
♦ Q43
♣ J7

North	East	South	West
1 ♦	Pass	1 ♠	2 ♣
2 ♠	Pass	4 ♠	All Pass

West cashed two high clubs and led a low club at trick three, hoping for an uppercut. When partner trumped with the eight of spades, that promoted an extra trump trick for west with the AT2.

One final piece of advice on uppercuts and trump promotion: Before you try for a trump promotion, **make sure that your side cashes all of your side suit winners first**. If you do not cash all of your side suit winners, declarer can sometimes counter the trump promotion by pitching a loser instead of overruffing. Here is an illustrative example:

DLR: South   ♠ Q75
VUL: N-S   ♥ KQ63
Matchpoints   ♦ J75
                ♣ KQ5

♠ JT6		♠ 9
♥ A42		♥ J9875
♦ AKQT62		♦ 83
♣ 8		♣ T9763

                ♠ AK8432
                ♥ T
                ♦ 94
                ♣ AJ42

South	West	North	East
1 ♠	2 ♦	3 ♦	Pass
4 ♠	All Pass		

West cashes the ace and king of diamonds. If west tries for an uppercut prematurely by leading a low diamond at trick three, declarer can simply pitch his heart loser when east ruffs with the nine of trumps, avoiding the uppercut. The winning defense is for west to cash the ace of hearts at trick three and then try for the uppercut by leading a low diamond at trick four – this promotes a trump trick for west and ensures beating the contract. In order for any type of trump promotion to be effective, **you must cash your side suit winners first.**

KEY POINTS

1. When there will be a long, strong side suit in the dummy, or when suits will be breaking well for the declarer, you must follow an active defense and go after your tricks before they go away. If dummy does not appear likely to have a long side suit, and declarer's suits will be breaking badly, you should defend passively and not give anything away.

2. The attitude signal that you give your partner on opening lead should be attitude towards the entire hand, not just towards the suit that was led. By using the Obvious Shift principle, you can tell your partner whether or not to shift to dummy's weak suit.

3. You should signal suit preference by the size of the spot cards that you play, in order to tell partner where your strength is.

4. When partner leads an obvious singleton against a suit contract and you cannot win the trick, the size of your spot card should be a suit preference signal, indicating your entry to give partner his ruff.

5. There are three occasions when a trump lead is called for:

   a) Partner passes your takeout double at the one- or two-level.
   b) The opponents are sacrificing against your game.
   c) Declarer has bid two suits, dummy takes a preference to the second suit, and you have length and strength in declarer's first bid suit.

6. When dummy has a four-card suit, or declarer has shown a four-card suit in the bidding, and you also have four cards in that suit, it is generally right to maintain parity and hold on to all four cards in this suit.

7. When you have trump length, you frequently want to lead your side's long side suit, forcing the declarer to ruff and lose control of the hand. This is known as the forcing game.

8. Your side can develop tricks in the trump suit by a trump promotion or an uppercut. Make sure that your side cashes all of your side suit winners first, or else declarer can use a loser on loser play to avoid losing an extra trump trick.

9. When declarer ruffs a side suit that you are also void in, you can frequently gain a trump trick by discarding a side suit loser instead of overruffing.

DEFENSE QUIZ

1. None Vulnerable, you hold:

	RHO	You	LHO	Partner
♠ T5	1♠	Pass	2♦	Pass
♥ K984	3♦	Pass	3♠	Pass
♦ J3	4♠	Pass	Pass	Pass
♣ JT943		What is your opening lead?		

2. Non-vulnerable versus Vulnerable, you hold:

	LHO	Partner	RHO	You
♠ 75	1♠	Pass	2♣	Pass
♥ 972	2♠	Pass	4♠	Pass
♦ 932	Pass	Pass		
♣ KJ965				

Partner leads the jack of hearts, and this dummy appears:

♠ Q2
♥ AKQ
♦ 876
♣ QT874

What heart do you play on this trick, and why?

3. Both vulnerable, you hold:

	Partner	RHO	You	LHO
♠ 982	1♥	Pass	Pass	DBL
♥ 964	Pass	1♠	Pass	1NT
♦ 8432	Pass	Pass	Pass	
♣ A94				

Partner leads the seven of hearts, and this dummy appears:

♠ QJ763
♥ T2
♦ QT96
♣ T7

Declarer wins the ten of hearts in dummy, and leads the three of spades at trick two. What spade do you play on this trick, and why?

4. None Vulnerable, you hold:

	Partner	RHO	You	LHO
♠ KQJ7	1NT	3♦	DBL*	Pass
♥ J972	Pass	Pass		
♦ 4				
♣ A976			* Negative	

What is your opening lead?

5. Vulnerable versus non-vulnerable, you hold:

	LHO	Partner	RHO	You
♠ T752	1NT	2♥	3♥*	Pass
♥ 93	3NT	Pass	Pass	Pass
♦ JT97				
♣ 765			* Stayman	

Partner leads the king of hearts, and this dummy appears:

♠ AQ93
♥ 764
♦ 54
♣ KQJT

Declarer ducks the first round of hearts and wins the ace of hearts on the second round. Declarer now runs four rounds of clubs. What do you discard on the fourth club?

6. None Vulnerable, you hold:

	RHO	You	LHO	Partner
♠ J3	Pass	Pass	1 ♦	Pass
♥ AKQ5	1 ♠	Pass	3 ♠	Pass
♦ T72	4 ♠	Pass	Pass	Pass
♣ J843				

You lead the queen of hearts, and this dummy appears:

♠ 8765
♥ 743
♦ AKQJ
♣ AK

You continue with the ace and king of hearts, and everybody follows. What do you play at trick four?

ANSWERS

1. **You must lead a heart** in order to take your tricks before they go away. Dummy has advertised a long, strong diamond suit, and you know that the diamonds are breaking for the declarer. You must employ an active defense. The full hand might be:

```
                    ♠ AQ3
                    ♥ T65
                    ♦ AQ875
                    ♣ 85
        ♠ T5                        ♠ 742
        ♥ K984                      ♥ AQ7
        ♦ J3                        ♦ 962
        ♣ JT943                     ♣ K762
                    ♠ KJ986
                    ♥ J32
                    ♦ KT4
                    ♣ AQ
```

If you don't lead a heart, declarer draws trump, pitches two heart losers away on dummy's good diamonds, and takes a successful club finesse to make twelve tricks.

2. **You should play the seven of hearts** to encourage hearts. Obviously, you don't have anything in hearts when dummy holds the AKQ, but you cannot stand a shift to dummy's weak suit, diamonds. Playing a high heart tells your partner not to shift to a diamond, which is exactly the message you want to convey.

3. **You should play the two of spades**, as suit preference for clubs, the lowest ranking suit. Count in spades is irrelevant – you must tell your partner where your entry is, so that partner can put you in to lead a heart through

declarer's KJ. If your entry were in diamonds, you should play the nine of spades to tell partner where your entry is.

4. **You should lead your singleton trump.** Your side has most of the points, and the opponents are sacrificing against your game. In order to take all of your tricks, you must prevent the declarer from crossruffing the hand and making tricks with dummy's trumps. The full hand may be:

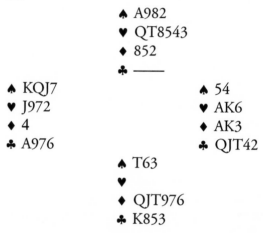

♠ A982
♥ QT8543
♦ 852
♣ ——

♠ KQJ7   ♠ 54
♥ J972   ♥ AK6
♦ 4   ♦ AK3
♣ A976   ♣ QJT42

♠ T63
♥
♦ QJT976
♣ K853

On a trump lead, declarer is held to five tricks, and your side scores +800, more than making up for the value of your vulnerable game. On the king of spades lead, declarer is able to ruff three clubs in dummy, and only goes down one trick.

5. **You must discard a diamond and keep all four of your spades.** If you throw a spade away, dummy's fourth spade becomes high whenever declarer holds the king of spades, which is a virtual certainty on the bidding.

6. With no side suit winners available in the minor suits, **your only chance to set the contract is to develop a trump trick.** Lead the thirteenth heart – if your partner holds the queen of spades, he will play it, and you will have developed the setting trick via an uppercut.

CHAPTER 8

MATCHPOINT STRATEGY

A. <u>Matchpoint Doubles</u>

Doubling a contract at matchpoints involves different considerations than doubling at Rubber Bridge or IMP's. The primary reason for doubling the opponents at matchpoints is **to protect your own partscore**. For example, if your side could have made seven or eight tricks in notrump for +90 or +120 and the opponents compete and bid 2♠, you must double them (or compete further) to try to get a score that is higher than your partscore would have been. If your double backfires and the opponents make their contract for a top, do not despair – you were getting a poor score anyway for going – 110 when most of the other pairs in your direction were recording plus scores on the hand.

This double to protect your own partscore, known as a "matchpoint double", is particularly lucrative when the opponents are vulnerable. Setting the opponents one trick in this situation results in attaining the magic figure of +200, which is higher than almost any partscore your side could have made. When the opponents are not vulnerable, you will sometimes find that you must beat their doubled contract by two tricks in order to get a good score. Nevertheless, even beating the opponents' contract one trick for +100 is better than being pushed one level too high and going minus on the board. Your side will generally still get some matchpoints for recording a plus score.

Doubling the opponents when they go berserk and bid a game when they should be in a partscore or bid a slam when they should be in a game is ego gratifying, but this type of double does not swing a lot of matchpoints to your side. When it is the opponents' hand, any plus score your way will give your side an excellent matchpoint result. It is when your side could have made something that doubling the opponents becomes mandatory.

Here are some examples of matchpoint doubles:

DLR: West   ♠ Q9632
VUL: None   ♥ T65
Matchpoints   ♦ T96
             ♣ 92

♠ J8   ♠ K754
♥ AJ943   ♥ Q87
♦ KQ3   ♦ A852
♣ QJ4   ♣ 53

           ♠ AT
           ♥ K2
           ♦ J74
           ♣ AKT876

South	West	North	East
	1♥	Pass	2♥
3♣	Pass	Pass	DBL
All Pass			

With a maximum 2♥ bid, east makes a **cooperative double** over south's 3♣ bid. This double shows a maximum 2♥ bid and asks partner to do something intelligent. It would be losing tactics to bid 3♥, allowing the opponents to push your side to the three-level when your side has only eight trumps. On this hand, west passes the double with a natural trick in the opponent's suit, and 3♣ doubled goes down three. Even down two would be a good result, **as long as the contract is doubled** – this beats the partscore in hearts that other pairs would be making.

DLR: West   ♠ KT53
VUL: N-S   ♥ AKJ
Matchpoints   ♦ JT76
                   ♣ 87

♠ 86   ♠ AQJ942
♥ T42   ♥ 87
♦ AKQ   ♦ 95
♣ AT653   ♣ J42

                   ♠ 7
                   ♥ Q9653
                   ♦ 8432
                   ♣ KQ9

South	West	North	East
	1♣	DBL	2♠
3♥	Pass	Pass	DBL
All Pass			

East made a matchpoint double of 3♥ because **he expected to make 2♠, so he doubled to protect his partscore.** On the lie of the cards, E-W can make nine tricks in spades for +140, but they got an even better result of +200 for beating 3♥ one trick. Notice that if N-S are allowed to play 3♥ undoubled, they will go down one for –100, beating all the E-W pairs who made a partscore in spades.

DLR: East
VUL: E-W
Matchpoints

♠ 62
♥ KT653
♦ 32
♣ J953

♠ QJ53
♥ QJ7
♦ T964
♣ 72

♠ AK74
♥ 842
♦ K5
♣ AQT8

♠ T98
♥ A9
♦ AQJ87
♣ K64

South	West	North	East
			1NT
2♦	DBL	All Pass	

It is not just when you have a good hand that you should make a matchpoint double — **it is whenever your side could have made a partscore.** Despite his poor hand, west realized that the hand belonged to his side for a partscore in notrump. West therefore made a penalty double of 2♦, hoping to get a higher score than the notrump partial available to his side. West led the queen of spades, holding the trick, and shifted to a trump at trick two to the king and ace. A second spade was won by east, who played his remaining trump, preventing a spade ruff in dummy. Declarer eventually lost three spade tricks, two clubs and one diamond for –200 and a top score for E-W.

B. Protecting Tenaces

It is frequently important to steer the contract to a particular hand in order to protect tenaces. A **tenace** is a broken honor sequence, such as AQ or KJ. In deciding whether to be the declarer or try to get partner to be the declarer in a particular contract, this concept of protecting tenaces becomes of paramount importance. If you have tenaces to protect, you should strive to become the declarer; on the other hand, if you have no honors to protect, you should try to get your partner to declare the hand. Here is a typical example:

DLR: South
VUL: E-W
Matchpoints

```
              ♠ 976
              ♥ K32
              ♦ 953
              ♣ AT65

♠ QT32                        ♠ 54
♥ Q87                         ♥ AJ54
♦ KQ42                        ♦ JT87
♣ 93                          ♣ KJ2

              ♠ AKJ8
              ♥ T96
              ♦ A6
              ♣ Q874
```

South	West	North	East
1♣	Pass	1♦*	Pass
1NT**	All Pass		

* Denies a four-card major unless he has game-forcing values
** Can have one or two four-card major suits

With two unprotected suits, north elected to get his partner to be the declarer by responding 1♦ instead of 1NT. N-S were playing inverted minors, so north could not bid 2C. N-S were also playing Walsh, where a 1♦ response denied a four-card major unless the responder had game-going values, and can be made on as few as three diamonds. This had the desired effect when south rebid 1NT. On a spade lead, south was able to make seven tricks by playing on clubs for a top score. Played from the north hand, 1NT goes down on a diamond lead.

Here is another example of protecting tenaces:

DLR: North   ♠ AKQJ2
VUL: E-W   ♥ QJ2
Matchpoints   ♦ JT82
             ♣ 8

♠ T83   ♠ 54
♥ 754   ♥ T96
♦ AK6   ♦ 54
♣ K654   ♣ JT9732

               ♠ 976
               ♥ AK83
               ♦ Q973
               ♣ AQ

North	East	South	West
1♠	Pass	2♦	Pass
3♦	Pass	3NT	All Pass

Despite a known eight-card spade fit, south wanted to be the declarer **to protect his club tenace**. In notrump, eleven tricks are there for the taking; in 4♠, the defenders can take the ace and king of diamonds and a diamond ruff. Even if the defenders do not find their diamond ruff, playing the hand in notrump results in a superior matchpoint score.

Here is an example of a slam hand that had to be played from the right side of the table to protect a king:

DLR: North
VUL: Both
Matchpoints

       ♠ A82
       ♥ AKT632
       ♦ 75
       ♣ KQ

♠ J54   ♠ T63
♥ J75   ♥ 4
♦ AQ32   ♦ J9864
♣ JT7   ♣ 5432

       ♠ KQ97
       ♥ Q98
       ♦ KT
       ♣ A986

North	East	South	West
1♥	Pass	1♠	Pass
3♥	Pass	4NT	Pass
5♦*	Pass	6NT	All Pass

* 0 or 3 keycards

Notice that 6♥ played by north goes down on a diamond lead. Despite holding three cards in his partner's suit, south bid 6NT **in order to protect the king of diamonds**, and was rewarded with a top score.

DLR: West
VUL: E-W
Matchpoints

```
              ♠ A72
              ♥ 92
              ♦ AKT754
              ♣ A7

♠ KJ3                        ♠ QT85
♥ AJT875                     ♥ Q64
♦ 92                         ♦ QJ6
♣ 98                         ♣ J53

              ♠ 964
              ♥ K3
              ♦ 83
              ♣ KQT642
```

South	West	North	East
	2♥	3♦	3♥
3NT	All Pass		

South bid 3NT in order to protect the king of hearts, hoping that either clubs or diamonds would run. On a heart lead, declarer made ten tricks when clubs broke 3–2.

```
DLR: North              ♠ 98
VUL: Both               ♥ 42
Matchpoints             ♦ AKJ753
                        ♣ KQT

   ♠ AQT654                              ♠ 7
   ♥ A7                                  ♥ QT86
   ♦ T2                                  ♦ 9864
   ♣ A83                                 ♣ J742

                        ♠ KJ32
                        ♥ KJ953
                        ♦ Q
                        ♣ 965
```

North	East	South	West
1 ♦	Pass	1 ♥	1 ♠
2 ♦	Pass	2NT	Pass
3NT	All Pass		

Although south had only ten points, he didn't want to put his hand down as dummy and get a spade lead through his KJ, so he made the slight overbid of 2NT **in order to protect his spade tenace.** North had an easy 3NT bid, and when west led a spade, declarer was able to make nine tricks by playing west for the ace of hearts.

Finally, here is a spectacular example of protecting the king, where one player bid notrump **despite having four-card support for his partner's suit:**

DLR: West   ♠ QT763
VUL: E-W   ♥ 932
Matchpoints   ♦ KQ
               ♣ AK3

♠ 5   ♠ KJ4
♥ AQT865   ♥ 7
♦ 76   ♦ JT8432
♣ JT96   ♣ 752

                ♠ A982
                ♥ KJ4
                ♦ A95
                ♣ Q84

South	West	North	East
	2♥	2♠	Pass
3♥	Pass	3♠	Pass
3NT	All Pass		

If north declares 4♠, east leads his singleton heart, and the defenders take the queen of hearts, the ace of hearts, and a heart ruff. East eventually makes the king of spades for down one. On a heart lead, 3NT made eleven tricks, and is unbeatable on any lead.

C. <u>Matchpoint Tactics</u>

There are certain principles that apply particularly to matchpoints. The first principle is that **whenever you have a long running minor suit, you should strive to get to 3NT.** Do not worry about the lack of stoppers in unbid suits – if you have a running minor suit and a stopper in the opponent's suit, just bid 3NT.

Have you ever thought about the difference between the following two auctions?

AUCTION A   AUCTION B
1♣-1♠-2NT   1♣-1♠-3NT

When the opener jumps to either 2NT or 3NT, **both of these jumps in notrump show 18-19 high card points.** The difference is that the jump to 3NT shows a minor suit source of tricks, while the jump to 2NT shows a balanced hand without a source of tricks.

Suppose you hold: ♠ AT6
               ♥ A
               ♦ 742
               ♣ AKQJ43

You open 1♣, your partner responds 1♥, and it is your rebid. With eight tricks in your own hand, **you should jump to 3NT at your second turn.** It is true that the opponents may be able to take the first five diamond tricks, but bridge is a game of percentages, and the odds are in favor of partner being able to contribute one trick, which is all you need to make 3NT. Note that your jump to 3NT does not preclude slam – it shows a source of tricks in the club suit and a good hand. If partner also has a good hand, he should bid on over your 3NT call.

Suppose your RHO opens 1♣, and you hold:

♠ Q6
♥ 54
♦ AKQJT75
♣ K8

You should **jump to 3NT** with this hand and not even mention your solid diamond suit. You have seven tricks in your own hand, and if you get the expected club lead, you are up to eight tricks. It is not too much to ask for partner to be able to contribute one trick in order to make a game in notrump.

The time to play in five of a minor suit is **when you have a distributional hand,** such as the following:

DLR: East
VUL: Both
Matchpoints

♠ 982
♥ J
♦ KT92
♣ KT852

♠ JT764
♥ 52
♦ A854
♣ 97

♠ AKQ5
♥ KT876
♦ 763
♣ 3

♠ 3
♥ AQ943
♦ QJ
♣ AQJ64

South	West	North	East
			1♥
2♣	Pass	3♣	Pass
5♣	All Pass		

With a distributional 5-5 hand, south jumps to 5♣, which is the only game that makes for his side.

You should especially want to bid 3NT when the opponents make a preemptive bid, and you hold stoppers in that suit. You will be able to shut out the preemptor, who has a long suit and very few high card points, and you will be able to develop tricks in the other suits. Suppose you hold:

♠ AQ9
♥ 2
♦ AT7
♣ KQJT85

If your RHO opens 2♠, you should jump to 3NT with your double spade stopper and your good club suit. Do not worry about the singleton heart – your partner is a huge favorite to hold heart length. Since there are only four spades outstanding between the other two players, and you hold length in clubs, you should play your partner for length in hearts.

Suppose you hold: ♠ K3
                              ♥ A4
                              ♦ Q87
                              ♣ AKT874

If your RHO opens 3♠, you should bid 3NT. You are hopeful of running six club tricks, you have the ace of hearts, and the spade opening lead will give you an eighth trick. **Do not make the mistake of overcalling 4♣ with this hand** – this bid bypasses 3NT, your likeliest game, and is a very inflexible action.

Here is a spectacular example of bidding 3NT with a long minor suit:

DLR: South   ♠ KQ87
VUL: Both   ♥ 72
Matchpoints   ♦ K6543
                        ♣ J5

♠ T9   ♠ AJ543
♥ AQT9864   ♥ K
♦ 982   ♦ QJT7
♣ 2   ♣ T93

                        ♠ 62
                        ♥ J53
                        ♦ A
                        ♣ AKQ8764

South	West	North	East
1♣	3♥	DBL	Pass
3NT!	Pass	Pass	Pass

Over partner's negative double, south took a chance and bid 3NT with his good seven-card club suit, despite not having a heart stopper. Partner didn't have a heart stopper either, but due to the blocked position of the hearts, 3NT proved to be unbeatable. This position is not uncommon, since most players do not have a solid suit when they preempt at the three-level. Remember the basic principle: **With a long strong minor suit, strive to bid 3NT.**

A second principle that applies to IMP's and Rubber Bridge, as well as matchpoints, is: **Strive to bid notrump with slow cards in the opponent's suit.** Aces and kings in the opponent's suit are more oriented towards suit play.

Suppose your partner opens 1♦, your RHO overcalls 1♠, and you hold either of the following hands:

HAND A	HAND B
♠ QJT3	♠ AK43
♥ AT5	♥ QT5
♦ A93	♦ Q93
♣ QJ6	♣ QJ6

You should jump to 3NT with either of these hands, but Hand A is much better for notrump play than Hand B. On Hand A, if the opponents lead spades, **you will use three of your points** to take two spade tricks; on Hand B, **you have to use seven of your points** to take the same two tricks. Another way of stating this principle is that secondary cards in the opponent's suit (queens and jacks) are very desirable for play in notrump, whereas primary cards in the opponent's suit (aces and kings) are not desirable.

Suppose you hold: ♠ KQT
                       ♥ 3
                       ♦ AK65
                       ♣ AQJ82

You open 1♣, your LHO overcalls 1♠, your partner makes a negative double, and your RHO jumps preemptively to 3♠. Since you have secondary cards in the opponent's suit and you do not fit your partner's heart suit, you should just bid 3NT. If there is a slam on this hand, you need your partner to make another bid over your 3NT call.

Here are two examples of bidding notrump with slow cards in the opponent's suit in the context of a complete hand:

DLR: East   ♠ T
VUL: None   ♥ KT9
Matchpoints   ♦ 643
            ♣ AKQJ96

```
        ♠ T
        ♥ KT9
        ♦ 643
        ♣ AKQJ96
♠ QJ8542          ♠ 6
♥ Q76             ♥ 853
♦ ——              ♦ AJT98752
♣ 8753            ♣ 2
        ♠ AK973
        ♥ AJ42
        ♦ KQ
        ♣ T4
```

South	West	North	East
			4♦
DBL	Pass	6♣	Pass
6NT	All Pass		

Holding KQ doubleton of diamonds, south felt that the same twelve tricks would be available in notrump as in 6♣, so he corrected 6♣ to 6NT. South played the non-preemptor for the queen of hearts to make 6NT, and was rewarded with a top score, as 6♣ goes down one on the ace of diamonds lead and a diamond ruff.

DLR: East   ♠ K7
VUL: Both   ♥ AQJT65
Matchpoints   ♦ T942
              ♣ 6

```
        ♠ QT8642                      ♠ J3
        ♥ K82                         ♥ 4
        ♦ 7                           ♦ AK863
        ♣ J84                         ♣ AT953
```

           ♠ A95
           ♥ 973
           ♦ QJ5
           ♣ KQ72

TABLE 1				TABLE 2			
South	West	North	East	South	West	North	East
			1♦				1♦
Pass	1♠	2♥	3♣	Pass	1♠	2♥	3♣
4♥	All Pass			3NT	All Pass		

When this board was played in a team game, the south player at Table 1 passed over east's 1♦ opening, and when his partner freely bid 2♥ over west's 1♠ response, he jumped to 4♥, figuring that he had a great hand for his partner.

East led the ace and king of diamonds and continued with the three of diamonds **as suit preference for clubs**. West ruffed, returned a club to his partner's ace, and a fourth round of diamonds enabled west to score the king of trumps for the second undertrick, +200 for N-S.

At Table 2, south followed the principle of **bidding notrump with slow cards in the opponent's suits**, and bid 3NT after hearing his partner overcall 2♥. With the king of hearts onside, this contract was cold, for a gain of 13 IMP's. North's diamond length, which was a distinct liability playing this hand in hearts, proved to be a major asset when the hand was played in notrump.

A third matchpoint principle to follow is to **prefer to bid 1NT rather than a poor five-card major suit or a good five-card minor suit if your bid may end the auction.** This way, if you play the hand in a partscore, you will be playing in the highest scoring partscore, rather than in the lowest scoring partscore (minor suit) or in a poor suit.

Suppose you hold the following hand:

        ♠ KJT

        ♥ Q3

        ♦ T8763

        ♣ AJ4

You pass in first seat, your LHO passes, and your partner opens 1♥ in third seat. Whatever you do, **do not bid 2♦** with this hand. Since you are a passed hand, your bid is non-forcing. If partner passes your 2♦ bid, you will be playing in the lowest scoring partscore with a poor suit. You should jump to 2NT with this hand – if partner passes your bid, you will be playing it in the highest scoring partscore instead of in a minor suit. An alternative bid would be to respond 1NT (non-forcing, since you are a passed hand) – if partner passes your 1NT bid, he has a minimum opening hand, and you haven't missed anything.

Suppose you hold: ♠ 2

                    ♥ J8542

                    ♦ AJ5

                    ♣ A973

You pass, your LHO opens 1♦, your partner overcalls 1♠, and your RHO passes. **Do not bid 2♥ with such a poor suit** – if your partner leaves you to play it there, you may be in a poor contract if your partner has heart shortness. It is much better to bid 1NT, which shows values and a stopper in the opponent's suit.

Here is an example of this principle in the context of an entire hand:

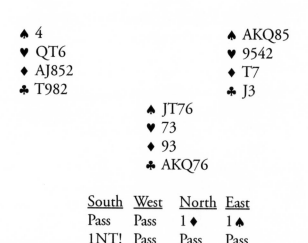

DLR: South
VUL: None
Matchpoints

♠ 932
♥ AKJ8
♦ KQ64
♣ 54

♠ 4
♥ QT6
♦ AJ852
♣ T982

♠ AKQ85
♥ 9542
♦ T7
♣ J3

♠ JT76
♥ 73
♦ 93
♣ AKQ76

South	West	North	East
Pass	Pass	1♦	1♠
1NT!	Pass	Pass	Pass

Instead of bidding 2♣, which would have ended the auction, south elected to bid 1NT and suppress the minor suit. Playing in 2♣, the limit of the hand is nine tricks for +90. Playing in notrump, declarer can take at least eight tricks by simply ducking the first round of clubs for a superior matchpoint score.

A well-known bridge principle is that **when the opponents preempt against you, stay fixed.** Staying fixed means not attempting to reach the optimal contract with limited bidding space, but trying to get to a reasonable spot. It means not stretching to bid a game or a slam because of the opponent's interference. You should realize that when one of the opponents preempt when your side has most of the high card points, **your suits will tend to break badly** for you. A 3-2 break in a side suit, which is normally a 68% chance, is no longer 68% when one of your opponents preempt. A

4-1 break, and even a 5-0 split, becomes much more likely when one of the opponents has a long suit.

Here is an example of "staying fixed":

DLR: East	♠ K63
VUL: N-S	♥ QT2
Matchpoints	♦ AK86
	♣ Q43

♠ 8	♠ JT52
♥ 43	♥ K87
♦ QT	♦ J7432
♣ AK987652	♣ T

♠ AQ974
♥ AJ965
♦ 95
♣ J

South	West	North	East
			Pass
1♠	4♣	4♠	All Pass

Over west's 4♣ preempt, north elected to "stay fixed" and just bid 4♠, not risking getting too high to explore for a possible slam. Although twelve tricks are possible, it requires a successful heart finesse and a finesse of the nine of spades on the second round of trumps!

DLR: East   ♠ KT
VUL: N-S   ♥ K97
Swiss Teams   ♦ AQJ942
                       ♣ J3

♠ J964   ♠ 82
♥ 542   ♥ AQT863
♦ T3   ♦ 865
♣ AQ98   ♣ T6

                ♠ AQ753
                ♥ J
                ♦ K7
                ♣ K7542

	TABLE 1				TABLE 2		
South	West	North	East	South	West	North	East
			2♥				2♥
2♠	3♥	4♦	Pass	2♠	3♥	3NT	Pass
4♠	Pass	Pass	Pass	Pass	Pass		

An important bridge principle when the opponents preempt
is **games before slams**. Do not try for slam if you risk going down
in a game. On this hand, the north player at Table 1 tried for slam
by bidding his diamond suit at the four-level, and ended up in 4♠
down one on a heart lead and a club shift. The north player at
Table 2 was willing to "stay fixed" and just bid 3NT, making ten
tricks for a pickup of twelve IMP's.

D. Third Seat Openings

When you are in third seat, your priorities are different than they are in first or second seats. In the first two seats, your priority is to have a constructive auction to get to your side's best contract. In third seat, if you have less than an opening hand, your top priority is **to disrupt the opponent's bidding**.

If there are two passes to you, there are several bids you can make in third seat to disrupt the opponents. You can open a weak two bid with a good five-card suit, or a weak three bid with a six-card suit. In third seat, you should prefer to open a good four-card major suit rather than a poor minor suit, even with an opening hand. Opening a good four-card major suit is a very effective tactic in third seat, as long as you have a good four-card suit that you want your partner to lead, such as AKJx or KQTx.

If you open light in third seat at the one-level, **the suit that you open must be lead-directional**. There is no reason to open light with a suit such as Qxxx – you don't have an opening bid, and you don't want your partner to lead this suit. If you open light in third position and your partner responds in a new suit or in notrump, **you must pass at your second turn**. Bidding again shows a full opening bid.

Here are some examples of third seat openings:

♠ AKJ94   **Open 2♠**
♥ 852
♦ 963
♣ 64

♠ 852   **Open 3♦**
♥ 7
♦ KQJT64
♣ K85

♠ 75   Open 1♥
♥ AQJ9
♦ Q52
♣ K643

Here are some examples of third seat openings in the context of an entire hand:

DLR: South   ♠ KJ85
VUL: Both   ♥ AKQ6
Matchpoints   ♦ T4
                        ♣ 653

♠ T76   ♠ 432
♥ J932   ♥ 84
♦ Q6   ♦ K98753
♣ KQJT   ♣ A7

                        ♠ AQ9
                        ♥ T75
                        ♦ AJ2
                        ♣ 9842

South	West	North	East
Pass	Pass	1♥	Pass
2NT	Pass	Pass	Pass

In third seat, north did not want to open 1♣ with three little clubs, so he opened 1♥ with his good four-card suit. With two good four-card majors in third seat, **you should always open 1♥**. This gives you room to find a heart fit, and also enables your side to find a spade fit if your partner responds 1♠. Opening this hand 1♠ makes it difficult to find a heart fit.

With 4-3-3-3 distribution, south elected to jump to 2NT rather than support hearts. The defenders took four clubs and a heart for a top score for N-S.

DLR: East   ♠ A5
VUL: Both   ♥ AK6
Matchpoints ♦ A9
      ♣ KJ6543

♠ KQT94   ♠ 73
♥ 4   ♥ QJ832
♦ 76542   ♦ T83
♣ A9   ♣ QT2

      ♠ J862
      ♥ T975
      ♦ KQJ
      ♣ 87

South	West	North	East
			Pass
Pass	2♠!	DBL	Pass
3H	Pass	3♠	Pass
3NT	All Pass		

N-S had a nice auction to play 3NT **from the right side of the table,** and the contract made when the clubs divided favorably. However, if north makes the mistake of bidding 3NT at his second turn, a spade opening lead defeats the contract.

DLR: East   ♠ KQ962
VUL: Both   ♥ AKT3
Matchpoints   ♦ T
                             ♣ T73

    ♠ AJ   ♠ T84
    ♥ 6   ♥ 974
    ♦ K98764   ♦ AQJ52
    ♣ K965   ♣ 42

                             ♠ 753
                             ♥ QJ852
                             ♦ 3
                             ♣ AQJ8

South	West	North	East
			Pass
Pass	2♦	DBL	5♦
5♥	All Pass		

In third seat, west opened 2♦ and found his partner with five-card support. 5♦ doubled would have gone down one, but south not unreasonably bid 5♥. When the club finesse failed, 5♥ went down one for a top score for E-W.

It is so important to disrupt the opponent's bidding when you are in third seat that you sometimes open with a preemptive bid **with opening bid values**. For example, if there are two passes to you and you hold:

♠ 2
♥ 976
♦ AJ2
♣ AQJ743

You should open 3♣ to make it difficult for the opponents to find their major suit fit. Although you would open 1♣ in first or second seat, once your partner is a passed hand, you know that your side does not have a game, and you want to make life difficult for your opponents. By varying your preempting style in third seat, you become a less predictable and a more dangerous opponent.

Here is another example of preempting with an opening hand:

DLR: West   ♠ Q54
VUL: E-W   ♥ T875
Matchpoints   ♦ A6
                ♣ J842

♠ J983   ♠ AKT762
♥ A63   ♥ KJ9
♦ KQ97   ♦ J85
♣ 93   ♣ 7

                ♠ ——
                ♥ Q42
                ♦ T432
                ♣ AKQT65

South	West	North	East
	Pass	Pass	1♠
3♣	4♠	5♣	Pass
Pass	DBL	All Pass	

At favorable vulnerability, south preempted to 3♣ facing a passed hand. When north competed to 5♣ with club support, N-S found a great save against the opponent's cold vulnerable 4♠ game.

KEY POINTS

1. The purpose of doubling the opponents at matchpoints is to protect the partscore that your side could have made if the opponents had not competed further. This "matchpoint double" is particularly lucrative when the opponents are vulnerable, as +200 is higher than almost any partscore your side could have made.

2. It is frequently important to play the contract from one side of the table in order to protect vulnerable honors, or tenaces. When you have tenaces to protect, you should strive to become the declarer; with no tenaces to protect, you should try to get your partner to declare the hand.

3. Whenever you have a long, solid minor suit, you should strive to get to 3NT.

4. It is also desirable to bid notrump when you have slow cards (queens and jacks) in the opponent's suit which will eventually take tricks. Your length in the opponent's suit is a liability for playing in a suit contract, but is an asset for playing in notrump.

5. Prefer to bid notrump rather than bidding a poor five-card major suit or a good five-card minor suit, particularly when your bid may end the auction. If you are going to play the hand in a partscore, you would prefer to be playing in the highest scoring partscore rather than a minor or a poor major suit.

6. When the opponents preempt against you, "stay fixed". Do not attempt to reach the optimal contract with limited bidding space, just try to get to a reasonable contract. When one of your opponents makes a preemptive bid, your suits will tend to break badly, so you should bid more conservatively.

7. When you are in third seat, your top priority is to disrupt the opponents' bidding. You can open a weak two bid with a five-card suit, or open 1♥ or 1♠ with a good four-card suit. These actions can only be done when you are in third seat.

8. If you open light in third seat, the suit that you open must be lead-directional. There is no point in opening light in third position with a poor suit.

9. If you open light in third seat, you must pass at your next turn to bid. Bidding again shows a full opening bid.

10. It is so important to disrupt the opponent's bidding when you are in third seat that you sometimes open with a preemptive bid with opening bid values. Since partner is a passed hand, you are not interested in game, and you want to take bidding space away from your opponents.

BIDDING QUIZ

1. None Vulnerable, you hold:

	Partner	RHO	You	LHO
♠ J975	1♣	2♦	DBL	3♦
♥ AK83	Pass	Pass	?	
♦ 93				
♣ J64				

2. Non-vulnerable versus vulnerable, you hold:

	Partner	RHO	You	LHO
♠ 976	1♠	Pass	1NT*	Pass
♥ AQ83	2♦	Pass	?	
♦ J6				
♣ KJ84			*Forcing	

3. Vulnerable versus non-vulnerable, you hold:

	You	LHO	Partner	RHO
♠ K8	Pass	Pass	1♣	1♠
♥ Q93	?			
♦ T9732				
♣ AJT				

4. Both Vulnerable, you hold:

	Partner	RHO	You	LHO
♠ AT87	1♠	4♣	?	
♥ AK2				
♦ KJ53				
♣ 82				

5. None Vulnerable, you hold:

	LHO	Partner	RHO	You
♠ K54	1♥	1♠	Pass	?
♥ JT87				
♦ AJT5				
♣ K2				

6. Both Vulnerable, you hold:

	Partner	RHO	You
♠ 2	Pass	Pass	?
♥ 9764			
♦ A4			
♣ AKJ743			

ANSWERS

1. **Double again**, showing a repeat negative double with extra values. Since your partner opened the bidding in first position and you have nine points, your side has the majority of the high card points. Therefore, you cannot let the opponents declare this hand undoubled.

2. **Bid 2NT**. Although your side has an eight-card spade fit, it is preferable for you to be the declarer on this hand in order to protect your tenaces in clubs and hearts.

3. **Bid 1NT**. Remember that bidding notrump is preferable to bidding a weak five-card suit at the two-level, particularly when your bid may end the auction. The complete hands may be as follows:

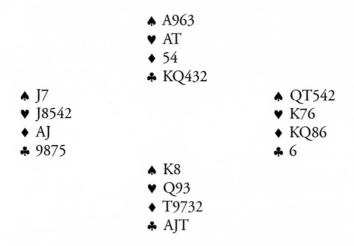

Notrump is a favorite to make nine tricks, which is a better score than playing this hand in clubs and making ten tricks.

4. **Bid 4♠** – When the opponents preempt against you, "stay fixed" and try to reach a reasonable contract. Without enemy interference, you would try for slam. Once the opponents preempt at a high level, you should realize that suits will not be breaking well for your side, and you should content yourself with bidding game.

5. **Jump to 2NT**, natural and invitational. Although your side has an eight-card spade fit, you have slow cards in the opponent's suit, which indicates that you should bid notrump. Your length in hearts, which is a liability playing in spades, will be an asset playing in notrump.

6. **Open 3♣** – Although you may have opened this hand 1♣ in first or second position, once your partner is a passed hand, your priority is to disrupt the opponent's auction. Opening 3♣ takes away the entire one- and two-level from the opponents. Since your partner is a passed hand, you are not interested in game, so you are free to open 3♣ with values.

CHAPTER 9

GREAT BRIDGE HANDS

I have played many bridge hands over the course of my bridge career. In this chapter, I will show you some of the greatest, wildest hands that I have been involved in. There was a statement attributed to the late great Victor Mitchell that "Bridge makes fools of us all", and these hands prove the validity of Mr. Mitchell's philosophy. I hope you enjoy looking at these hands for the first time.

NINETEEN-POINT SLAM

DLR: South   ♠ K2
VUL: None   ♥ QJ7632
Matchpoints   ♦ J8765
                    ♣ ——

♠ Q9853   ♠ J764
♥ K   ♥ T
♦ KQ32   ♦ T9
♣ QJ4   ♣ AK8763

                    ♠ AT
                    ♥ A9854
                    ♦ A4
                    ♣ T952

South	West	North	East
1♥	DBL	4♣!	4♠
DBL	Pass	5♣!	DBL
6♥	Pass	Pass	Pass

After a sequence in which north could not be accused of underbidding, south became declarer in 6♥ with a combined total of nineteen points between the two hands. After north had splintered in clubs, showing shortness, and then cuebid 5♣, showing first round control, south realized that all of his points were working and jumped to the slam. After the opening lead of the king of diamonds went to declarer's ace, declarer crossed to dummy with the king of spades and took the right view in hearts, playing the ace as west followed with the king. Declarer conceded a diamond trick for +980 and a top score.

BERGEN RAISE MISUNDERSTANDING

DLR: East
VUL: E-W
Matchpoints

	♠ 7432	
	♥ ——	
	♦ QT9764	
	♣ K75	
♠ K86		♠ AJ
♥ QT94		♥ AK8732
♦ J8		♦ 52
♣ AQ32		♣ JT4
	♠ QT95	
	♥ J65	
	♦ AK3	
	♣ 986	

East	South	West	North
1♥	Pass	3♦*	DBL
4♥	4♠	Pass	Pass
DBL	Pass	Pass	Pass

* Bergen Raise, 10-12 points and 4 trumps

North doubled west's Bergen raise of 3♦ to show diamonds, but his partner thought this was a takeout double of hearts, and jumped to 4♠. With trumps 3-2, the jack of spades onside, and diamonds 2-2, this contract only goes down one against the opponent's cold 4♥ game. The defenders were so flustered by the bidding, however, that they never attacked clubs, and declarer made his doubled contract.

THE WORLD'S GREATEST PSYCHE

DLR: South
VUL: N-S
Rubber Bridge

♠ —
♥ AKQT9764
♦ QJ964
♣ —

♠ AQJ93
♥ 5
♦ 732
♣ T864

♠ 8762
♥ J3
♦ 8
♣ AK9532

♠ KT54
♥ 82
♦ AKT5
♣ QJ7

South	West	North	East
1♦	1♠	2♣!	2♠
Pass	Pass	5NT*	Pass
7♦	DBL	All Pass	

* Grand Slam Force in diamonds

This sad but true story actually occurred in a high stakes rubber bridge game. North decided that he wanted to be in a grand slam if his partner held the ace and king of diamonds, so he psyched 2♣ in his void suit, **never mentioning his solid eight-card heart suit.** North eventually used the Grand Slam Force to get to 7♦, and east made a Lightner double, asking for the lead of dummy's first bid suit, clubs. West duly led a club, and declarer ruffed in dummy and claimed thirteen tricks for +2330.

PERFECT DEFENSE

DLR: East   ♠ QT643
VUL: Both   ♥ 7
Matchpoints   ♦ A42
                   ♣ KQ65

♠ AJ72   ♠ K95
♥ 654   ♥ AT2
♦ K5   ♦ T9876
♣ A942   ♣ T7

                   ♠ 8
                   ♥ KQJ983
                   ♦ QJ3
                   ♣ J83

East	South	West	North
Pass	2♥	Pass	Pass
Pass			

In Rubber Bridge or IMP's, preventing declarer from making overtricks in a contract is not very important, but at matchpoint duplicate, it is often the difference between a top and a bottom score.

With no attractive lead to make, west led a trump to his partner's ace. East shifted to the ten of clubs at trick two, **and west encouraged with the nine** as dummy's queen won the trick. A low spade was led to declarer's eight and west's jack, and west played ace of clubs and a club for his partner to ruff. East shifted to the ten of diamonds, covered by the jack, king and ace – this took out dummy's entry to the good club. Declarer played dummy's good club, but east ruffed with the ten of trumps, overruffed by the declarer. Declarer drew trumps, but had to concede a diamond trick at the end for +110 and a top score to E-W.

PLAYING IN GOOD FORM

DLR: West
VUL: Both
Rubber Bridge

<pre>
                    ♠ A9654
                    ♥ J852
                    ♦ Q74
                    ♣ 4
  ♠ QJ32   ♠ KT87
  ♥ K96   ♥ AQ4
  ♦ J65   ♦ 3
  ♣ KJ3   ♣ AT876
                    ♠ ——
                    ♥ T73
                    ♦ AKT982
                    ♣ Q952
</pre>

West	North	East	South
Pass	Pass	1 ♠	2 ♦
3 ♦	4 ♦	4 ♠	5 ♦
DBL	Pass	Pass	Pass

Playing Rubber Bridge with Zia is always fun and exciting. Zia has a way of loosening up the table, making it fun for everyone.

On this hand, the last of a four-deal Chicago, I found myself partnering Zia in the west seat. Zia has a knack for getting his opponents in trouble without them even knowing what is happening to them. On this hand, Zia didn't really have a 4♠ bid, but he knew his opponents, and figured that his opponents would take a "save" in 5♦ if he bid 4♠ — how right he was! I doubled the 5♦ contract, and it was my lead.

I led the five of diamonds, and dummy's seven of diamonds won the first trick. Declarer pitched a club on the ace of spades, as Zia followed with the king **to show hearts** and I followed with the two **to show clubs.** Declarer now led dummy's singleton club, and Zia **ducked his ace,** enabling me to win the jack and play another trump, won in dummy with the queen. Declarer now led a heart, and Zia **ducked again with the AQ of hearts,** enabling me to win the king and play my third trump. This led to down three and +800 for our side. After the hand was over, I complimented Zia on his superb defense of ducking both his ace of clubs and ace of hearts. Zia's answer to me was, "Thanks, but your hand was an open book". That's what makes Zia such a great bridge player.

MATCHPOINT REDOUBLE

DLR: South   ♠ 876532
VUL: None   ♥ AQ8732
Matchpoints   ♦ ——
           ♣ 2

♠ AJ9   ♠ ——
♥ K952   ♥ T6
♦ AKJ   ♦ QT87654
♣ Q96   ♣ J843

                 ♠ KQT4
                 ♥ J
                 ♦ 932
                 ♣ AKT75

South	West	North	East
1♣	1NT	2NT	Pass
3♠	Pass	4♠	Pass
Pass	DBL	RDBL	All Pass

It is extremely rare to need to redouble to get a good matchpoint score. Usually, if you make a doubled contract, your side will receive an excellent score.

This hand is an exception to the rule. 4♠ doubled, making four or five, was a common result on this hand, and the redouble was necessary to get a good matchpoint score.

North's bid of 2NT over west's 1NT overcall showed a **two-suited distributional hand**. N-S had never discussed this bid, but it is the only logical meaning for it. North cannot have a good hand, or he would have doubled 1NT for penalty. Therefore, 2NT must be a two-suited takeout.

When south bid 3♠, west hesitated before passing, obviously thinking about doubling 3♠. North observed this, and knew that west would certainly double 4♠. When he bid 4♠ and west doubled, he redoubled immediately, and taught west a sharp lesson. This is yet another example that high card points do not take tricks – distribution is what matters!

GOOD GAMBLE

DLR: South
VUL: Both
Matchpoints

North:
♠ J74
♥ ——
♦ AKQJ8
♣ K7632

West:
♠ 92
♥ AKT53
♦ 642
♣ Q98

East:
♠ T8
♥ QJ9876
♦ 753
♣ AT

South:
♠ AKQ653
♥ 42
♦ T9
♣ J54

South	West	North	East
2♠	Pass	2NT	Pass
3NT*	Pass	6♠	All Pass

* Solid six-card suit

When south showed a solid six-card spade suit by bidding 3NT over 2NT, north gambled out a 6♠ bid. There were many ways that 6♠ could be the winning action: The ace of clubs might be onside, or the defenders might not lead a club, or partner could have the jack of clubs or a singleton club. On the actual lead of the ace of hearts, declarer was able to ruff in dummy, cross to his hand with a diamond, ruff his other heart loser, and draw trumps and claim thirteen tricks, pitching his three clubs on dummy's three high diamonds.

ALL FOUR SUITS AT THE SEVEN-LEVEL

DLR: South	♠ 862
VUL: N-S	♥ 863
Matchpoints	♦ Q86
	♣ A742

♠ 5		♠ Q3
♥ 5		♥ Q74
♦ AJ932		♦ KT754
♣ KQ8653		♣ JT9

	♠ AKJT974
	♥ AKJT92
	♦ ——
	♣ ——

South	East	North	West
1♠	2NT	Pass	4♦
6♥	7♣	Pass	7♦
7♥	Pass	7♠	All Pass

South had an impossible hand to bid, and made a good effort by opening 1♠ and jumping to 6♥ when the opponents competed in the minor suits. East, looking at favorable vulnerability and what he thought was one defensive trick, competed to 7♣, and partner corrected to 7♦. South decided to allow the opponents to push him into the grand slam, and bid 7♥, which his partner corrected to 7♠. This is the only auction I have ever seen where **all four suits were bid at the seven-level**.

Declarer ruffed the ace of diamonds opening lead, drew trumps in two rounds, and cashed the ace of hearts. He was now able to get to dummy with the eight of spades, and the grand slam depended on whether or not he guessed the heart suit correctly. Declarer went right by finessing east for the queen. He played west, who had shown length in the minors, for heart shortness. In addition, **west was unlikely to compete to 7♣ with Qx of hearts**. East was rewarded with +2210 and a top score.

UNDISCIPLINED WEAK TWO BID

DLR: South
VUL: E-W
Matchpoints

♠ JT543
♥ 4
♦ T8764
♣ 84

♠ A86   ♠ KQ9
♥ 9762   ♥ J53
♦ AJ2   ♦ KQ9
♣ KJ2   ♣ AQT7

♠ 72
♥ AKQT8
♦ 53
♣ 9653

South	West	North	East
2♥*	Pass	Pass	DBL
Pass	Pass	Pass	

* Undisciplined weak two bid

Imagine picking up seventeen high card points, hear your partner open the bidding, and discover that you can't even make a game. This is what generally happened on this board after west opened 1♣. Going down one in 3NT after south cashed his five heart tricks was an average result on this board.

At some tables, however, south opened 2♥ in first seat at favorable vulnerability. East reopened with an offshape takeout double, and west passed for penalties with values and no suit to bid. South took his five heart tricks for –500 **and a complete bottom on the board.**

ROMAN KEYCARD BLACKWOOD DISASTER

DLR: North
VUL: Both
Swiss Teams

♠ AKQJ764
♥ AQJT5
♦ ——
♣ A

♠ T9832
♥ 862
♦ 54
♣ T83

♠ 5
♥ 7
♦ 8732
♣ KQJ9765

♠ ——
♥ K943
♦ AKQJT96
♣ 42

North	East	South	West
2♣	3♣	3♦	Pass
4NT	Pass	5♠*	Pass
5NT	Pass	7♦	Pass
7♠	Pass	Pass	Pass

* 2 keycards and the queen of trumps

When north bid 4NT, south responded Roman Keycard Blackwood for diamonds and bid 5♠, showing two keycards and the queen of trumps. When north bid 5NT, **guaranteeing all of the keycards**, south jumped to 7♦ and passed when his partner corrected to 7♠. Justice was served when 7♠ went down one due to the 5-1 trump break. Note that N-S are cold for 7♦, 7♥ and 7NT!

The funniest part of this story is that this hand was played in a team game, **and the board was a push!** Both sides bid the only grand slam that didn't make!

This hand illustrates the error of using Roman Keycard Blackwood before you have decided upon the trump suit.

CRUCIAL OPENING LEAD

DLR: North   ♠ QJ96
VUL: N-S   ♥ ——
Swiss Teams   ♦ AJ543
                  ♣ AT65

♠ T8   ♠ 5
♥ K543   ♥ QT976
♦ Q876   ♦ KT2
♣ Q32   ♣ K987

            ♠ AK7432
            ♥ AJ82
            ♦ 9
            ♣ J4

North	East	South	West
1♦	1♥	1♠	2♥
4♥*	Pass	4NT	Pass
5♠**	Pass	7♠	All Pass

* Splinter bid in support of spades
**2 keycards and the queen of trumps

South was able to count thirteen tricks if partner held either minor suit king, and would at worst be on a finesse if partner held either minor suit queen, so he bid the grand slam.

The success or failure of the grand slam hinges upon west's opening lead. If west leads either red suit, declarer has the entries to set up dummy's fifth diamond to pitch his losing club and make the slam. On a black suit lead, one of dummy's entries is used prematurely, and declarer cannot set up and use dummy's fifth diamond, and must go down one.

West actually led a heart, his partner's suit, and declarer went +2210 instead of −100.

INDEX

Active and Passive Defense 186-190, 208-209
Balancing 100-106
Baze, Grant 47
Cansino, Jonathan 18
Cansino Count 18, 20
Cohen, Larry 9, 76
Combining Chances 156-160
Competitive Bidding 85-90
Cooperative Double 78, 111, 125-129, 233
Counting 150-156
Deception 161-166
Double Game Swing 38, 43, 48
Dummy Points 130
Final Guess 77, 88-90
Fit Showing Jump 99-100
Forcing Defense 211-214
Four-Three Fit 175-177
Granovetter, Matthew & Pamela 9, 190
Help Suit Game Try 97-98
Law of Total Trumps 44, 59, 76-81, 137
Loser on Loser Play 170-175, 215
Mahmood, Zia 9, 11, 269-270
Maintain Parity 209-210
Matchpoint Double 232-235
Matchpoint Tactics 242-252
Miles, Marshall 9, 60
Misfits 38, 44-46

Mitchell, Victor 264
Negative Doubles 112-116, 118-119
Obvious Shift Carding 190-197
Overcalls 25-28
Passed Hand Bidding 96-100
Picture Bidding 81-85
Protecting Tenaces 93-94, 235-241
Raising With 3-Card Support 60-65
Reopening Double 116-118, 143
Responding Light 66-67
Responsive Doubles 119-124
Restricted Choice 166-170
Reverse Drury 97-99
Roth, Alvin 81
Rule of Eleven 64
Safety Play 160
Schenken, Howard 218
Six-Five, Come Alive 50,56,116
Stay Fixed 250-252
Suit Preference Defense 198-203, 248
Support with Support 39-43, 56, 96, 107
Takeout Doubles 129-144
Third Seat Openings 253-257
Trump Promotion 172, 214-220
Unusual Finesses 153-154
Unusual Notrump 51-53
Uppercut 221-224
Walsh 236
Weak Two Bids 21-24, 272, 274
Woolsey, Kit 9, 88, 128